Prayer - A Deeper Understanding
(Taking Your Prayer Life to the Next Level)

Ps 19:14

14 Let the words of my mouth, and the meditation of my heart, be acceptable in thy sight, O LORD, my strength, and my redeemer.
KJV

Biblical
TEACHER

Samuel Williams

Prayer - A Deeper Understanding
(Taking Your Prayer Life to the Next Level)

To order additional copies, visit,
www.createspace.com/8186987

http://samuelkem.wixsite.com/truthaboutthetithe
Contact the author via email at samuelkem@aol.com.

Printed by Createspace an Amazon.com company
Printed in the United States of America 2018
First Edition

Unless otherwise indicated all Scripture quotations are taken from the King James Version of the Holy Bible. Scripture quotations marked (NKJV) are taken from New King James Version. © 1979, 1980, 1982, 1984 by Thomas Nelson, Inc.

Contents

Introductions

The high majority of people do not have the full understanding of how important prayer is to their spiritual lives. When we take the time to comprehend the teachings and demonstrations of prayer in the Bible, we are actually learning the correct way to hold a conversation with the God of all things. In addition, I said, "conversation," because when we pray the proper way, God has promised that He hears us and will answer. He replies in many ways and in many time periods, but He will answer. Think about the joy that you received the first time you experienced God answering your prayer.

I was on Facebook one day watching a video of a little girl who was three or four years old running around praising God because He healed her. The mother asked the little girl what happened and she explained how she prayed to God as she was taught because she was sick. The little girl did not even pray correctly because she was taught the wrong way. It shows how God will overlook our ignorance while we grow in the knowledge of the truth. When we learn the truth, we are required to implement it. God saw the faith of this little girl and her innocence. He answered her petition. She asked God to heal her, and as soon as she finished praying, all the sickness went away. You could see by this little child's face that she was really healed. She ran around the room saying, "Halleluiah," so joyfully. When children experience God at such a young age, it is cemented in their hearts that God is real. These experiences do wonders in building a relationship between God and the child. Trust me when I say the reason you are reading this book is because God took notice of my first real prayer, and even when I was against Him as a young man, He remembered me. When we experience God in our lives, no one can tell us He is not real.

If you have yet to experience God, have no worries. If you follow the instructions from scriptures that I am going to share with you, God has promised He will manifest to you. If you pray correctly, then God will answer your prayer. It is a promise, and God keeps His promises.

When I began my vocation in the Body of Christ (as a teacher), one of the first lessons God gave me to teach was about prayer. Let me put it in a way that you can better understand. I have taught over a thousand Bible study lessons, and one of the first topics God gave me to teach was prayer. When I look back, I realize that God was setting the foundation of the relationship He wanted to build with me and with those He sent for me to teach. Learning the proper way to pray is paramount, as it enhances every other area of our spiritual life.

More than ninety percent of Christians do not know how to pray correctly. Sadly, the same misconceptions on praying are passed down to the children. Children learn how to pray by watching their parents. It is imperative that we teach our children the right way to pray from a young age. This will enable the truth on prayer to be passed down through them. What is the best way of getting your kids involved in prayer? Pray for them and with them!

Now my job as a teacher in the Body of Christ is to reveal to you the instructions on praying as laid out in scripture, and you will be able to share this knowledge. Do not feel reluctant to learn about praying. Most Christians believe they already know the proper way to pray. This book will be shocking because it is going to reveal many facets of praying that the average believer does not know. Yet when we take the time to learn them, they will assist us in our spiritual walk and growth. The purpose of this book is to reduce the time that it will take you to grow into a powerful praying Christian. For some this will take years off your spiritual growth. To achieve this we first have to be honest with God and ourselves, acknowledging that our prayers are seldom if ever answered. The Bible says that the fervent prayer of a righteous man avails much. So why are you not seeing the results of your prayers? God does not lie and the issue is never with Him, it is always with us. Therefore, if we can be honest with ourselves and say there is a deficiency in our prayer life, then it is the first step in dealing with the issue and removing the problem. God left a blueprint on proper prayer in the scriptures for all believers. There are many examples to learn from and many pieces to the puzzle. When we gather up all the pieces and put them together, we get a clear teaching on how to pray properly so that our prayers are heard and acted upon by God. Let's get started.

Chapter 1

The Basics

The Format Given by Christ for Praying

The disciples asked Christ to teach them how to pray and He gives the first in-depth teaching in scripture on praying. I am always amazed at how Christ can teach us how to do something, yet today we who confess that we are the followers of Christ seem to have so little knowledge of what He taught. We are sometimes more inclined to follow what we have learned from others than to go into the scriptures and learn what was left to us from our Lord and Savior.

The devil uses the lack of diligence to follow what Christ has commanded as a way of introducing antichrist propaganda and methods to hinder Christians. The enemy of our souls will actually interject the opposite of what Christ taught and many will accept it as the norm, oblivious to what Christ actually instructed.

The apostles also left us nuggets of understanding concerning prayer. These men learned directly from Jesus. In addition, all throughout the Old Testament we are shown examples of how men and women of God prayed. These examples give us a visual of the truth of how we as believers should be praying. The easiest way to identify the lie is to know and understand the truth. Let's investigate the truth of what the scriptures teach on praying.

Matt 6:5-15
5 And **when thou prayest, thou shalt not be as the hypocrites are: for they love to pray standing in the synagogues and in the**

corners of the streets, that they may be seen of men. Verily I say unto you, They have their reward.

6 But thou, when thou prayest, enter into thy closet, and when thou hast shut thy door, pray to thy Father which is in secret; and thy Father which seeth in secret shall reward thee openly.

7 But **when ye pray, use not vain repetitions,** as the heathen do: for they think that they shall be heard for their much speaking.

8 Be not ye therefore like unto them: for your Father knoweth what things ye have need of, before ye ask him.

9 **After this manner therefore pray ye:** Our Father which art in heaven, Hallowed be thy name.

10 Thy kingdom come. Thy will be done in earth, as it is in heaven.

11 Give us this day our daily bread.

12 And forgive us our debts, as we forgive our debtors.

13 And lead us not into temptation, but deliver us from evil: For thine is the kingdom, and the power, and the glory, for ever. Amen.

14 For if ye forgive men their trespasses, your heavenly Father will also forgive you:

15 But if ye forgive not men their trespasses, neither will your Father forgive your trespasses.

KJV

Christ's Break Down on Prayer

Don't be a hypocrite

As Christians, we have to understand that our prayer is to commune with God and not with men. **We should never pray to impress people.** Have you ever noticed a person praying in front of a crowd whose vocabulary suddenly moves to a higher level than when they regularly speak? Ask yourself if they are trying to impress God or men. **God is not impressed by big words. He is impressed by the state of the heart and obedience.** Many people pray to impress the crowd, and Christ is showing in verse 5 that their reward will be the praise of men because God will give them nothing.

If you pay attention to prayers of this type, you will notice that the person is actually talking to the crowd, not God.

Example: Lord, some people around here are getting jealous because of how you are blessing me but if they would mind their own business and stay out of mine, maybe you would bless them also.

This is not a prayer to God; this is a person using prayer to address people. Over the years, I have heard many prayers where believers use a public prayer to address wrongs to the congregation, group, or individual. This is a total misuse of a sacred rite. Christ shows that our prayers should not be to attain praise from men but should be as if we are in our closet in a one on one with God. I like to tell people just to have a conversation with God. **Be honest and straightforward showing reverence.** When we do this, it enables us to pray an effective prayer.

Do not use vain repetitions

Try not to use vain repetitions. It is not about a prayer we have memorized; it is about what is going on that brings the need to talk to the Father. It is not about saying Hail Marys, which are nowhere in the scriptures. It is about addressing your needs and petitioning God on behalf of the present circumstances. If you notice a systematic pattern in your prayer, then you are praying wrong. Yes, there is a certain format that Christ left us to follow, but this is just a guide, it does not fit every circumstance. You might start your prayer in a familiar format to address the Father in Christ's name but the meat of the prayer should address the situation.

It is not about how long you pray. Long prayers do not increase your chances of being heard. Do we realize most of Christ's prayers in scripture are actually short? Before Christ was crucified, He prayed for the disciples and it was a 3-4 minute prayer. His prayer was one of the longest you will find in the scriptures.

Sidenote: There will be times when we just want to prostrate (lay flat on the ground) before God and just pour out our hearts to Him. To prostrate before God in prayer is scriptural. We find examples in scripture such as when David asked God for mercy concerning his newborn son. We see men and women of God doing this in time of great trouble. I have laid before God in times of trouble and prayed for what seems like hours, but it was less of what God needed to know and more of me needing to vent.

Peaceful Place

Sometimes it is necessary to pray in places where others are around or there is noise that we cannot control. However, when we can, we should find a quiet place to facilitate our conversation with God. Christ would go off by Himself and find a quiet place not because he needed to but because he was giving us an example of what we need to do.

Mark 1:35
35 And in the morning, rising up a great while before day, he went out, **and departed into a solitary place, and there prayed.**

Mark 6:46
46 And when he had sent them away, **he departed into a mountain to pray.**

We cannot always go off to the mountains to pray but I can tell you from experience that some of my best prayers were prayed out in nature and even in my back yard. When we are in a peaceful place surrounded by the things created by God, it is like a breath of fresh air that allows us to freely release to God.

Any quiet place where we are free from distraction can also facilitate prayer. Quiet rooms, closets (home/work), our cars, or even the attic of our homes can be used as a place of peace to talk uninterrupted to God.

Concentrate

The first step to saying our prayer is to concentrate on God. Clear out all other thoughts in your mind. We often pray to God while thinking about other things and the prayer is interrupted by our imagination. You know when you are praying and thinking about what you need to eat. (Do not be deceived, God sees the plate of pizza in your mind as you are trying to talk to Him.) Remember, the same effort you put forth in the prayer should be the same effort you expect in your answer. Thank God for His mercy because He often does not respond according to the effort that we give Him.

TEACH US TO PRAY

I want to address a tough issue about praying in the Christian church. **Christ's whole mission was to bring us back into relationship with the Father.** He told us to pray to the Father in Jesus' name. Are we following Christ's instructions or doing what we want to do? I want you to read this carefully:

John 16:22-28
22 Therefore you now have sorrow; but I will see you again and your heart will rejoice, and your joy no one will take from you.
23 "And in that day you will ask Me nothing. **Most assuredly, I say to you, whatever you ask the Father in My name He will give you. 24 Until now you have asked nothing in My name. Ask, and you will receive, that your joy may be full.**
25 "These things I have spoken to you in figurative language; but the time is coming when I will no longer speak to you in figurative language, but I will tell you plainly about the Father. 26 **In that day you will ask in My name, and I do not say to you that I shall pray the Father for you;** 27 for the Father Himself loves you, because you have loved Me, and have believed that I came forth from God. 28 I came forth from the Father and have come into the world. Again, I leave the world and go to the Father."
NKJV

Christ told the disciples that He was going to be crucified and they would be sorrowful because of His death. However, He also told them that when He is resurrected, then their sorrow would turn to joy that cannot be taken away from them. His death would pay the price for their sins and would allow them to regain a connection to the Father. This renewed connection with the Father by Christ's blood comes with many benefits. **One of the main benefits is a direct line to the Father through prayer.** Look closely at verse 23. Christ told the disciples that after the resurrection they would no longer ask Him anything because they now had access to the Holy of Holies in heaven. They had a direct line to the Father in Jesus' name (meaning salvation of God/ Yehoshua in Hebrew).

Saints, we are supposed to be praying to the Father in Jesus' name, not praying to Jesus in Jesus' name. I have heard many believers over the years who have tried to defend why they pray to Jesus in Jesus' name. I am not here to argue the point with you. I am here to give you the instructions left by Christ Himself on how we should pray. Jesus Christ our Lord and Savior, instructed us to pray to the Father in His name. Christ died so we can have access to the Father. If He told us to pray in this way it is for a reason, and we should never try to justify not following what He commanded. Yes, there are times I speak to Christ concerning something specific I want to know from Him but the high majority of my prayers are according to His instructions, which is to the Father.

Does it matter if we follow the instructions or not? I will share a point that the Holy Spirit spoke into my spirit. **God answers our prayers (sometimes) because of His mercy but He is NOT obligated to because we are praying in error.** When we pray correctly, God will answer our prayers. God is obligated to answer every single prayer prayed according to the instructions left for us in scripture. We will confirm this truth later in the book.

The disciples of Christ asked Him to teach them how to pray and this is the example He gave them that should serve as a blueprint for our prayers.

PRAISE and SUBMISSION

Matt 6:9-10
9 After this manner therefore pray ye: Our Father which art in heaven, Hallowed be thy name.
10 Thy kingdom come. Thy will be done in earth, as it is in heaven.
KJV

Christ taught us to start our prayers by embracing the Father as the true God that rules in heaven. The word "Hallowed" shows that God's name (Yah) in itself is holy. We then embrace the truth that His kingdom is going to be established on earth. His will is preeminent in both heaven and earth. These words are a form of praise and confessing that we submit to God's will. Address **the**

Father with praise showing reverence and knowing that scripture says that He inhabits the praise of His saints.

Ps 22:3
3 But thou art holy, O thou that inhabitest the praises of Israel.
KJV

Those that confess Christ, and are born again, will start noticing strange sensations over their body when they are sending up an effective prayer. Some will feel a tingling over their bodies that will start on their feet and move up. I want you to do this the next time you pray. **I want you to spend extra time praising and glorifying God and pay attention to what you feel.**

You will also need to lineup in the other areas that you will be taught in this book. Other things can hinder our prayers. An example is your prayer not being heard because of unforgiveness in your heart (much on this later).

When we take time and really praise God, we can feel His presence around us. First our spirit feels like it is charging up in anticipation of God's presence and then we feel the power of God moving in us and around us. It is true that He inhabits the praise of His people so always start your prayer with praise.

Example: Oh great and mighty God, the Creator of all things, Your Word says that heaven is thy throne and earth is thy footstool. Who is like You, oh God, who inhabits eternity? From everlasting to everlasting, You are God and there is none like thee. By Your breath is all life and You sustain all things. Hallelujah, hallelujah, hallelujah. Glory, honor, and power be unto Your name. Your will is established in heaven and in the earth, let it also be established in my life. I bless Your holy name.

Now that we have learned how to get God's attention, we move into the area of what we need from Him. Christ addressed this but like He often does, He hid the deeper meaning by using a natural understanding.

Download daily knowledge

Matt 6:11
11 Give us this day our daily bread.
KJV

One of the things that I love about Christ's Words is the fact that there is often a deeper meaning than what is on the surface. When He taught the disciples to pray, He showed that they should ask the Father to give them their daily portion of bread. In the natural, this pertains to food but it has a deeper meaning. The spiritual food of God's Word is issued to each believer on a daily basis, if we are paying attention. God is always speaking but we are not always paying attention to the spiritual bread of His Word being distributed to believers. Let's take a look at some scriptures that confirm this.

Job 23:12
12 Neither have I gone back from the commandment of his lips; **I have esteemed the words of his mouth more than my necessary food.**
KJV

Matt 4:4
4 But he answered and said, It is written, **Man shall not live by bread alone, but by every word that proceedeth out of the mouth of God.**
KJV

When I first became a teacher in the Body of Christ, I noticed that God would give me a weekly lesson to teach to His children. Shortly after, I started realizing that He was also giving me daily lessons for my personal growth. It was very subtle at first but as I started to expect the Word and pay more attention, the daily inspiration placed into my spirit became more noticeable. Everyone in the Body of Christ gets this but many miss it because they are not paying attention or do not realize it is God sending them a message.

Have you ever gone to church, heard the pastor preach, and then heard a similar message on the radio? Later the same message you received comes up in the conversation with friends. When you went to Bible study, the teacher spoke on what you just finished talking about. This takes place when the Holy Spirit is relaying a message from God into the Body and it will resonate among the members. **In the same way, when God has a message for us, we will hear it multiple times throughout the day/week until we get it, IF we are paying attention.** Understand that the answers to our prayers will often come this way also.

You will listen to someone and they will talk about something that has been on your mind. You will read a scripture and a word in the verse will catch your attention and then you will hear the very same word spoken on the TV or radio. I even know a friend that God deals with by sending her messages on cars' license plates. We get our daily bread in many ways. As we mature in our Christian walk, we will more readily recognize the Holy Spirit's daily ministering into our hearts and the weekly messages for the Body of Christ.

Sidenote: The weekly bread or knowledge that is ministered to the Body of Christ is symbolized by the shewbread that was placed in the holy place of the Temple. The priest would place twelve loaves of bread on the table in the holy place. The twelve loaves represented the twelve tribes of Israel and they were renewed (replaced) every seven days. To have access to this bread, you have to position yourself in the spiritual holy place, which we will discuss more thoroughly later in the book.

What I will share with you now is that if you read and meditate on His Word throughout the day, you will never miss your share of this daily bread. God feeds all His children and His meals are spiritually nutritional words containing all we need for spiritual growth. It is up to us to determine if we miss the meal or not. When we petition Him to give us this daily spiritual bread, He makes sure we don't miss it when it comes forth. Glory be to God.

I also love that in the daily bread, God will also point out corrections we need to make in our Christian walk. If we are walking in sin, He will bring it up in our daily portion of spiritual bread. We will feel convicted by the Word coming forth. When this happens, it is up to us to embrace the truth and repent. This is why scripture teaches that we receive everything from God, which we need to make it into the kingdom. **Never resist correction that is truth.** Do not try to justify rejecting correction because it is not to harm us, it is our friend.

Prov 8:33-34
33 Hear instruction, and be wise, and refuse it not.
34 Blessed is the man that heareth me, **watching daily at my gates**, waiting at the posts of my doors.
KJV

When it comes from God, it has no other purpose than to point us in the direction of holiness. This is why Christ in His example addresses correction in the next part of His instructions on prayer.

Forgiveness

Matt 6:12
12 And forgive us our debts, as we forgive our debtors.
KJV

Many people believe that God accepts all prayers but this is not correct.

Ps 66:18
18 If I regard iniquity in my heart, the Lord will not hear me:
KJV

Before we can approach God with our petition (request) we need to clear up our sins by repenting before Him. Be honest because God already knows the situation. He just wants you to address it and ask for forgiveness (and/or mercy) and repent (turn from the sin) before you ask Him for something. I want you to understand this: If you get in trouble with your parents for doing something wrong and refuse to acknowledge it (say you're sorry), and turn away from what you were doing that was wrong, you can't go and ask them to buy you a car. Sin brings separation and repentance brings us back into right standing. **Never let the enemy deceive**

you into thinking you cannot repent before God. Pray for forgiveness and mercy if needed. There is only one sin that God will not accept prayer for (sin unto death), and we will go over it later in the book.

Pray and confess because the enemy knows that as long as he can keep you in a sinful state, the better chance he has of getting you to give up your walk in Christ. When Christ taught that we should forgive those that have trespassed against us that come and ask for forgiveness, up to seven times in a day, He was teaching the ways of God.

Luke 17:3-4
3 Take heed to yourselves. If your brother sins against you, rebuke him; and if he repents, forgive him. 4 And if he sins against you seven times in a day, and seven times in a day returns to you, saying, 'I repent,' you shall forgive him."
NKJV

The Father does the same when we come to Him earnestly in repentance. If you are a studier of the Old Testament (all believers should be), then you know how many times God forgave Israel. God knows our weakness and does not want us to give in to the sin. He wants us to wage battle against it, but if we fall we are to get up and continue the battle immediately. If you sin, pray a prayer of repentance without delay, asking for forgiveness and God will forgive. If you allow the devil to fool you into not asking for forgiveness, then sit, and wallow in the sin, judgment will fall on you. Once judgment falls because of procrastinating to ask for forgiveness of the sin, then you should ask for mercy in the judgment. The longer we wait to clear up the sin, the deeper we will sink in the pit of the enemy and the harder it will be to get out.

It is good to be ashamed of the sins we have committed but do not let this stop you from going before the mercy seat. Satan will try everything at his disposal to maintain your position in the sin because as long as you are there he has access to you. That is why scripture tells us to go boldly to the throne of grace:

Heb 4:14-16
Seeing then that we have a great High Priest who has passed through the heavens, Jesus the Son of God, let us hold fast our confession. 15 For we do not have a High Priest who cannot sympathize with our weaknesses, but was in all points tempted as we are, yet without sin. 16 Let us therefore come boldly to the throne of grace, that we may obtain mercy and find grace to help in time of need. NKJV

Example: Father, I ask for forgiveness for all my unconfessed sins, the lust of the flesh, the lust of the eyes, and the pride of life. Forgive me for sins that I have committed knowingly and unknowingly, sins of omission and commission. Father forgive me for every thought and imagination that has raised up against the knowledge of your Word. In addition, Father I forgive all those that have wronged me in anyway according to Your Word.

We are instructed to ask the Father to forgive our debts (sins) that we owe Him and it is on condition that we also forgive those who sin against us. This is a powerful revelation. I go deeper into the act of unforgiveness later in the book but for now, I want you to understand that if we do not forgive others on a daily basis, then we are wasting our time asking God for forgiveness. Just as God's mercy towards us is on condition that we also show mercy to others and the same type and degree of mercy, we show others will be exactly what we receive from God. For those who like to hold things against others even after they ask for forgiveness, please know that you are killing yourself spiritually. If you do not forgive, you will not be forgiven, period.

Please do not slip on this. Do you realize that after Christ completed His example of praying, **He doubled back and addressed forgiveness again?** This demonstrates how important it is that our Lord and savior goes back to reaffirm that it is paramount that we forgive others.

Matt 6:14-15
14 For **if ye forgive men their trespasses, your heavenly Father will also forgive you:**

15 But **if ye forgive not men their trespasses, neither will your Father forgive your trespasses**.
KJV

I want to add a note of warning. Do not take God's mercy for granted. Remember Israel's example, if we continually embrace sin we will be judged and judgment has degrees that can even result in death. Respect God's mercy and do not abuse it.

Now that you have access, ASK for what you need

Matt 6:13
13 And **lead us** not into **temptation**, but **deliver us** from **evil**: For thine is the kingdom, and the power, and the glory, for ever. Amen.
KJV

Christ's example reflects a sheep following the Shepherd (Christ) who leads His sheep safely. Do you realize that Christ will have the Holy Spirit prompt you when you are wandering from the fold? You do realize that every fold has some hardheaded sheep. During the day, if we are paying attention, the Holy Spirit will let us know when temptation is coming our way and the pitfalls of temptation that are setup to entrap us. Mature believers will feel the prompting of the Holy Spirit because through experience we have become used to it.

Deeper Understanding of Watch and Pray

Matt 26:36-44
Then Jesus came with them to a place called Gethsemane, and said to the disciples, "Sit here while I go and pray over there." 37 And He took with Him Peter and the two sons of Zebedee, and He began to be sorrowful and deeply distressed. 38 Then He said to them, "My soul is exceedingly sorrowful, even to death. Stay here and watch with Me."
39 He went a little farther and fell on His face, and prayed, saying, "O My Father, if it is possible, let this cup pass from Me; nevertheless, not as I will, but as You will."
40 Then He came to the disciples and found them sleeping, and said to Peter, "What! Could you not watch with Me one hour? 41 Watch

and pray, lest you enter into temptation. The spirit indeed is willing, but the flesh is weak."

42 Again, a second time, He went away and prayed, saying, "O My Father, if this cup cannot pass away from Me unless I drink it, Your will be done." 43 And He came and found them asleep again, for their eyes were heavy.

44 So He left them, went away again, and prayed the third time, saying the same words.

NKJV

Christ was not tempted to go against the Father's will when He said, "Not my will, but thine, be done." He told the apostles to "watch and pray," but watch what, and pray for what? It was nighttime, and they were in a garden on the Mount of Olives. He already knew the authorities were coming for Him and when they would get there, so what did He want the apostles to watch for? Christ wanted the apostles to watch Him and then pray the words He was going to pray. He knew that they would be tempted to give up and would need to do exactly what He was showing them.

Christ told the disciples to pray that they do not enter into temptation. Luke noted in his version of the story that an angel came and strengthened Christ. Christ told them their flesh was weak, they needed strengthening. We as believers have to watch what Christ did and learn from it. Do you realize that most people pray after they have gone through the temptation and have already failed? Have you ever wondered if Peter would have followed Jesus' instructions and prayed as Jesus prayed that perhaps he would have been strengthened also, enabling him to stand by Jesus' side rather than denying him and fleeing? Prayer to the Father is a form of humbling ourselves, even as we bow down and acknowledge Him as the true and living God. We say, "Father, not our will but let your will be done," then He will send an angel to strengthen us so that we also can have the ability to do what He has willed for us to do.

Now let me open your eyes to a gem hidden in the story. Did you notice that God's will and not being led into temptation is part of the format given by Christ to the disciples on how to pray (Matt 6:9-13)? When Christ prayed, He emphasized that it was all about God's will (the very same thing that He emphasized to the disciples on how to start their prayer "Thy will be done")

Christ came back and found the disciples sleeping. He wakes them and again instructs them to watch Him and to pray because He knew temptation was coming their way because of His crucifixion. Christ knew that they would be tempted to give up. The Shepherd was instructing the sheep to keep their eyes on Him and follow His footsteps (do as He does).

The Shepherd will also be there to protect the sheep from every danger that comes along but our level of protection is determined by our close proximity to the Shepherd. We have to stay close to Christ. **The key to staying close is to walk in obedience and to stay fixated on Him.** Keep your mind stayed on the things of God.

Before you make a decision, check to see if your choice draws you away from your protection, which is Christ. The temptation will come after your own desires draw you away from the Shepherd. It will attempt to pull you out of Christ.

James 1:14
14 But each one is tempted when he is drawn away by his own desires and enticed.
NKJV

Always check to see where the Shepherd is before you move. If your next move draws you out of the fold (away from Christ's doctrine), reject it for a choice that keeps you close to God. Understand that the enemy we face is crafty and often works through deception. We pray (communicate with God) so that we can tell Him what we feel, what we need, and hear His instructions on what we need to do.

Do not be Anxious, Present your decisions before God and His Word, before they are finalized.

Phil 4:6

6 Be anxious for nothing, but in everything by prayer and supplication, with thanksgiving, let your requests be made known to God;

NKJV

Paul is explaining that we should not be anxious and rush into anything but we are to pray before we make a decision. We must invite God into our decisions to obtain His guidance. We thank Him even before He replies, trusting that He will answer our petition and guide us into the right decision. **Never let the enemy push you into making a decision on important matters without first taking it up with God. Also, never let the enemy tell you the matter is not important enough to check with God.** God is interested in all facets of our lives and is pleased when we come to Him for guidance.

Have you ever been in a situation where you did not want to pray to God about something because you knew what you wanted was wrong or that you thought He might say, "no"? Do you trust God to do what is best for you? Now, ask yourself, "Do I really trust God?"

God will give us everything we need and He will also grant our desires if they do not take us out of His will. God wants the best for us and we need to trust Him. When we do not trust Him, we will allow the lust of the flesh, the lust of the eyes, and the pride of life to war against us. This lust will push us to do anything to obtain what we know we cannot ask from Him. Some will even be pushed to ask for things that the Word of God teaches that we cannot have.

James 4:2-4

2 You lust and do not have. You murder and covet and cannot obtain. You fight and war. Yet you do not have because you do not ask. 3 You ask and do not receive, because you ask amiss, that you may spend it on your pleasures.

NKJV

We have to understand that we must also ask according to God's will to assure that we receive our request. **We cannot ask for things that violate God's will for us or others and believe that the prayer will be answered and we will receive our request.** Many times people pray for things that the Word of God says we can't get or that just violates the Word. If you are praying for the spouse of someone else to be yours, you are wasting your time. If you are praying for something that will cause you to sin, you are wasting your time. If you are praying for things to consume through your lust, you are wasting your time. God does not want us to waste our prayers on things to fulfill our lustful desires, which will hinder us from making it into the Kingdom.

God said He would give us the desires of our heart but too many times, we are asking for the desires of our flesh and wandering why we do not receive them. God is talking about walking with a pure heart according to the hidden man of the heart, which is a meek and quiet spirit. The spirit man, which is Christ in us, does not desire vain things from God.

Job 35:13
13 Surely God will not hear vanity, neither will the Almighty regard it.
KJV

Prov 21:13
13 Whoever shuts his ears to the cry of the poor
Will also cry himself and not be heard.
NKJV

Isa 1:15-17
15 When you spread out your hands,
I will hide My eyes from you;
Even though you make many prayers,
I will not hear.
Your hands are full of blood.
16 Wash yourselves, make yourselves clean;
Put away the evil of your doings from before My eyes.
Cease to do evil,
17 Learn to do good;
Seek justice,

Rebuke the oppressor;
Defend the fatherless,
Plead for the widow.
NKJV

Zech 7:12-14
12 Yes, they made their hearts like flint, refusing to hear the law and the words which the LORD of hosts had sent by His Spirit through the former prophets. Thus great wrath came from the LORD of hosts. 13 Therefore it happened, that just as He proclaimed and they would not hear, so they called out and I would not listen," says the LORD of hosts.
NKJV

Trust God, He wants the best for His children. Trust Him.

Pray to the Father giving worship in Jesus' name! Ask for daily knowledge (bread) of what He needs you to know. Ask for forgiveness, so your prayer is not hindered by unconfessed sin. Also, at the same time make sure you have forgiven others so that your forgiveness is granted. Petition the Father with your request. Praise God with thanksgiving. End your prayer in Jesus' name and amen.

When to Pray

Many of the great men of the Bible had a pattern of praying at least twice a day. It is common to teach that a person should pray upon waking up to start the day and before laying down to sleep for the night.

Ps 119:147-148
147 I rise before the dawning of the morning,
And cry for help;
I hope in Your word.
148 My eyes are awake through the night watches,
That I may meditate on Your word.
NKJV

Our morning prayers should come with scripture reading and a period of devotion. This is important to prepare our minds for the trials and tribulations of the day and to also manifest the things God has spoken into our spirit during the night. Yes, God talks to us in the nighttime as we sleep.

Job 33:14-16
14 For God may speak in one way, or in another,
Yet man does not perceive it.
15 In a dream, in a vision of the night,
When deep sleep falls upon men,
While slumbering on their beds,
16 Then He opens the ears of men,
And seals their instruction.
NKJV

Remember that prayer is a conversation with God where we are asking Him for the things we need to maintain ourselves in Christ, the necessities for this life, and protection from our enemies. What many people miss is that the Bible also teaches that we need to pray throughout the day.

Ps 55:17
17 **Evening, and morning, and at noon**, will I pray, and cry aloud: and he shall hear my voice.
KJV

Anytime we feel the unction in our spirit, we should take a few minutes to send up a prayer. Many times, we do not even recognize what we need to pray about but as we walk in obedience to what we are feeling in our spirit, God will reveal the reason as we start praying. Sometimes it is for us to avoid traps of the enemy and other times to intercede on the behalf of others.

Eph 6:18
18 praying always with all prayer and supplication in the Spirit, being watchful to this end with all perseverance and supplication for all the saints —
NKJV

I could share countless testimonies of God waking me and telling me to pray for a family member or a brother or sister in Christ.

Many times, I will find out later that there was a situation going on in their lives at that very moment and they were desperately in need of prayer. I have also had others tell me that God woke them up to pray for me and they would be spot on because I was going through something at the time.

Ps 119:62-63
62 At midnight I will rise to give thanks unto thee because of thy righteous judgments.
63 I am a companion of all them that fear thee, and of them that keep thy precepts.

I have a very close friend that God will frequently prompt to pray for me when I am going through struggles. She will often mention it to me and the timing will be right on time. Often she will get the unction to pray for me when I am fighting in my attempts to pray. God sees our struggles. He will notify spiritually those in Christ that are close to us to intercede on our behalf.

Even during the writing of this book, I had a friend call me and say he was speaking to another friend and kept calling him by my name. His wife said, "You need to call Sam," and sure enough I was experiencing an inner struggle, which happens as the enemy attempts to hinder the teachings God has me working on. Sometimes as ministers of the Gospel, it is hard to share what we are going through and in truth, it is also the same with most believers. The Holy Spirit will have prayer warriors fight the battle for us as we regain our footing in the fight.

Standing in the Gap

1 Tim 2:1-4
2:1 I exhort therefore, that, first of all, supplications, prayers,
intercessions, and giving of thanks, be made for all men;
2 For kings, and for all that are in authority; that we may lead a quiet
and peaceable life in all godliness and honesty.
3 For this is good and acceptable in the sight of God our Saviour;
4 Who will have all men to be saved, and to come unto the
knowledge of the truth.
KJV

God searched for someone to stand in the gap for Israel. People believe standing in the gap means to stand between the individual and the enemy, but this is not what scripture teaches. **Standing in the gap means you are interceding on your brother or sister's behalf to stop God's judgment.** Many times in our Christian life, we will see our brethren playing with fire, and God wants us to pray them through their walk in foolishness. We all go through it, and it is not for us to wish them to fall so we can say, "I told you so."

Ezek 22:30
30 And I sought for a man among them, **that should make up the hedge, and stand in the gap before me for the land, that I should not destroy it:** but I found none.
KJV

Many times spiritually immature Christians want their brothers to fall, especially if they have been hurt by them in some way. This is when you can differentiate the mature walking in love and the babes walking in a fleshly carnal mind. We are to want the best for our brothers and sisters no matter what they have put us through because we understand we are all in the same fight for our souls. **So even if you hurt me, if I see you falling, I will run to catch you.**

If as a Christian you have never prayed for, fasted for, and cried out to God for your brethren, then something is wrong with your understanding. We are a family, and we are obligated to lift one another up because (trust me) there will come a time when you will need lifting up yourself. When we are under attack, we want people to pray for us and intercede to God on our behalf. When we see others struggling, what kind of prayer do we send up for them? How many days do we fast for them? What effort do we show for them? **Do you understand that interceding for them is a form of mercy?** The Body of Christ is a family, and when we help others in the body, we are helping ourselves. Those who love mercy (and confirm this by showing it) will receive mercy when they are judged.

Scripture gives us many examples of men of God interceding for the people. Job, Moses, Hezekiah, David, and many more stood in the gap.

2 Chron 30:18-20
18 For a multitude of the people, many from Ephraim, Manasseh, Issachar, and Zebulun, had not cleansed themselves, yet they ate the Passover contrary to what was written. **But Hezekiah prayed for them, saying, "May the good LORD provide atonement for everyone** 19 who prepares his heart to seek God, the LORD God of his fathers, though he is not cleansed according to the purification of the sanctuary." 20 And the LORD listened to Hezekiah and healed the people.
NKJV

Ps 106:23
23 Therefore he said that he would destroy them, had not **Moses his chosen stood before him in the breach, to turn away his wrath, lest he should destroy them.**
KJV

Christ Himself was the leader in this matter, giving His life so that we all might live. No man could be found, so Christ came. The arm of the Lord was sent to stand in the gap.

Isa 63:5
5 And **I looked, and there was none to help; and I wondered that there was none to uphold**: therefore mine own arm brought salvation unto me; and my fury, it upheld me.
KJV

Did you notice that in each case the person was not intervening to stop Satan? They were interceding to stop judgment from God. **It should be sobering to realize that God is in control, yet He is a God of judgment and mercy.**

Sidenote: Here is message for parents; there will be times when you will need to stand in the gap for your children lest the wrath of God falls upon them. If you do not believe me, then your kids have not gotten to that teenage and young adult age as yet. Once you start dealing with them in that age group, you will change your mind. Life is full of stages, and in some, we walk close to the cliff, but **the prayers of loved ones are often the lifeline that keeps us from going over.**

Sin unto Death

The Bible speaks of one sin that we as believers are not to stand in the gap concerning our brothers/sisters in Christ.

1 John 5:16-21
16 If any man see his brother sin a sin which is not unto death, he shall ask, and he shall give him life for them that sin not unto death. **There is a sin unto death: I do not say that he shall pray for it.**
17 All unrighteousness is sin: and there is a sin not unto death.
18 We know that whosoever is born of God sinneth not; but he that is begotten of God keepeth himself, and that wicked one toucheth him not.
19 And we know that we are of God, and the whole world lieth in wickedness.
20 And we know that the Son of God is come, and hath given us an understanding, that we may know him that is true, and we are in him that is true, even in his Son Jesus Christ. This is the true God, and eternal life.
21 **Little children, keep yourselves from idols**. Amen.
KJV

There are a few misinterpreted verses in the scripture above. The first is verse 16 and the sin unto death. Many believers have been taught that the sin unto death is the blaspheming of the Holy Ghost. This is the type of misinterpretation that is running rampant through the church. It is taught from the pulpit, and no one questions it. When you line it up with scriptures and the proper understanding, you are exposed to the truth of the sin unto death.

Where in scripture does it say blaspheming of the Holy Spirit leads to death? Nowhere! So where does the concept come from?

29

Matt 12:31-32
"Therefore I say to you, every sin and blasphemy will be forgiven men, but **the blasphemy against the Spirit will not be forgiven men.** 32 Anyone who speaks a word against the Son of Man, it will be forgiven him; but whoever speaks against the Holy Spirit, it will not be forgiven him, either in this age or in the age to come.
NKJV

Here is where the misconception comes in. Christ said those who blaspheme the Holy Spirit would never be forgiven. What exactly does that mean? Before we deal with that, let's deal with what forgiveness means.

If you are forgiven for something, it means you will receive no punishment. If you receive punishment for a sin, and the punishment is cut short, this is not forgiveness it is mercy. **Forgiveness means no penalty, and mercy means the degree of the punishment is reduced even to the point of no penalty.** What Christ is saying is that if you blaspheme the Holy Ghost, you will receive punishment. There is no way that the punishment can be taken away. You will have to pay the price and receive judgment! Does this mean that you are going to hell? You have to realize that every single person that has ever lived on this earth will experience judgment. The difference between believers and unbelievers is that we are judged in this world for all post-baptismal sins that are not forgiven.

1 Cor 11:32
32 But **when we are judged, we are chastened of the Lord, that we should not be condemned with the world.**
KJV

When we sin (and are not forgiven), God brings judgment against us so that we can mature in holiness. Our chastisement (punishment) helps us to grow spiritually and put on the image of Christ.

Heb 12:10-14
10 For they verily for a few days chastened us after their own pleasure; but he for our profit, that we might be partakers of his holiness.
11 Now no chastening for the present seemeth to be joyous, but grievous: nevertheless afterward it yieldeth the peaceable fruit of righteousness unto them which are exercised thereby.
12 Wherefore lift up the hands which hang down, and the feeble knees;
13 And make straight paths for your feet, lest that which is lame be turned out of the way; but let it rather be healed.
14 Follow peace with all men, and holiness, without which no man shall see the Lord:
KJV

Sinners receive judgment at the end of the world and the punishment is the second death and eternal fire. **As believers, we are judged according to the mercy we show others. Therefore, even when we are judged, we determine the degree.** If you blaspheme the Holy Spirit, you will not be forgiven, you will receive judgment, and the degree is determined by the mercy you show others.

James 2:13
13 For he shall have judgment without mercy, that hath shewed no mercy; and mercy rejoiceth against judgment.
KJV

Therefore, even if you blaspheme the Holy Spirit and receive no forgiveness but a guaranteed judgment, it is not the sin unto death. Be warned, as Christians we are always judged according to the mercy we show others.

So what is the sin unto death? John told us, but most of us miss it. **"Little children, keep yourselves from idols," 1John5:21.** This revelation of the sin unto death is confirmed by carefully reading verse 16 and 21 of 1 John 5 (see pages 28,29). With the sin unto death (worshiping other gods), we are told if we see our brother or sister in this sin, we are not to pray for them. This is the only time where we do not stand in the gap for our brothers/sisters. **Other times, we are the lifeline between them and death.**

Jer 7:16-18

16 Therefore **pray not thou for this people, neither lift up cry nor prayer for them, neither make intercession to me: for I will not hear thee.**

17 Seest thou not what they do in the cities of Judah and in the streets of Jerusalem?

18 The children gather wood, and the fathers kindle the fire, and the women knead their dough, to make cakes to the queen of heaven, and to pour out drink offerings unto **other gods**, that they may provoke me to anger.

KJV

When we see our brothers/sisters knowingly worship other gods or idols after they have tasted of the gift of the Holy Spirit and eternal life, we are not to pray for them. They have committed the sin unto death.

I want to reiterate that this is one of the most important chapters in the book. You must understand the basics if you are to learn the proper way to communicate with God. Proper prayer will allow you to enter into His presence and will be a foundation stone of knowledge that will enable you to stand against the storms of wickedness in this world. You will develop a relationship with God that will be reinforced by the time you spend in the Holy Space in communion with Him. This shared time will build and increase your faith, and nothing will be able to shake your belief in God. Once you have experienced God, nothing and no one can convince you He does not exist. Now that we have the basics down let's move on to **the deeper things of PRAYER.**

Don't forget to teach your children to pray!

Chapter 2

God's House

I want to ask you a question! What was the purpose of the temple in scriptures?

Matt 21:13-14
13 And said unto them, It is written, **My house shall be called the house of prayer**; but ye have made it a den of thieves.
14 And **the blind and the lame came to him in the temple; and he healed them.**
KJV

What was Christ quoting from?

Isa 56:7
7 Even them will I bring to my holy mountain, and make them joyful in **my house of prayer**: their burnt offerings and their sacrifices shall be accepted upon mine altar; **for mine house shall be called an house of prayer for all people.**
KJV

The above scripture exposes how important prayer is to God. The very temple on earth where His presence dwells was called the House of Prayer. He is showing that this would be the purpose of His temple. The temple was not just to hear prayers but to answer them also. We see above where Christ healed people in the temple. Who can forget when Hanna kneeled in the Tabernacle and made a petition for a child? God answered her prayer with one of the greatest men of God in the Bible, Samuel!

Understand that prayer is communing with God, and the temple became a Sacred Place where God's Holy Space could meet with men. God's presence is a **Holy Space**, wherever it resides the area becomes a **Sacred Place**, and when we are in that place communing with God, we are operating in **Holy Time**. A Sacred Place, where God's presence (Holy Space) resides. Holy Time, when man meets with God at the Sacred Place in His presence (Holy Space).

God made the temple a Sacred Place where men could come to pray to Him even when He was chastising them.

2 Chron 7:12-16

12 And the LORD appeared to Solomon by night, and said unto him, I have heard thy prayer, and **have chosen this place to myself for an house of sacrifice.**
13 If I shut up heaven that there be no rain, or if I command the locusts to devour the land, or if I send pestilence among my people;
14 If my people, which are called by my name, shall humble themselves, and pray, and seek my face, and turn from their wicked ways; then will I hear from heaven, and will forgive their sin, and will heal their land.
15 **Now mine eyes shall be open, and mine ears attent unto the prayer that is made in this place.**
16 For now have I chosen and sanctified this house, that my name may be there for ever: and mine eyes and mine heart shall be there perpetually.
KJV

In the same manner, the garden was also a Sacred Place where the Holy Space of God came and met with Adam. When Adam and Eve rejected holiness, they were expelled from the Sacred Place where God's Holy Space resided. When Israel rejected holiness, it was a rejection of God. When this came to a head, it would always end with the removal of the Holy Space and then the destruction of the Sacred Place (temple). The only way Israel heard from God after this was when He sent a prophet or messenger angel.

They were in exile! What did God tell them to do when they found themselves in this situation?

Hos 5:15

15 I will go and return to my place, *till* **they acknowledge their offence, and seek my face: in their affliction they will seek me early.**
KJV

Do you realize that key parts of coming back into right relationship with God entails "turning from your wicked ways" and "acknowledging your offence"? Many of the false gospels out there today are telling believers that this is not necessary because of grace. This brings us to the question: Are we required to obey Christ's teachings? Yes, we are!

James 1:22

22 But be ye **doers of the word**, and not hearers only, **deceiving your own selves.**
KJV

When we accept any doctrine that tells us as hearers of the Word of God (as given by Christ) that it is not required that we obey it, then we have deceived ourselves. Believers are not those who just **hear** the Word, they also **keep** it.

Adam had dominion in the garden. He was instructed by God to take dominion over space and the things in space. When God gave mankind dominion over the earth, it was not so we could rule it according to how we see fit, but to control it so that it would function according to God's will. God had already placed His purpose in everything that was created. Adam's responsibility was to make sure it was working according to the purpose established by God. Adam had to follow God's instructions on how to have dominion over not just the earth, but also the Sacred Place God had set aside to commune with man. Adam was the high priest of the garden. Even as the overseer, Adam's instructions came from God. **Holiness was/is walking according to the instructions given by God.** For us as Christians, we must walk according to the instructions given by the Father to Jesus Christ for us. What is holiness simplified? **What Christ says to do, do it! What He says don't do, don't do it!**

God instructed Israel to pray and seek His face, but what did He mean by seeking His face? Israel was told that if they were in exile, they should pray towards the temple. If they were not in exile, then they would go to the temple to seek Him. Seeking Him is much more than just looking for Him.

Zeph 2:3
3 Seek ye the LORD, all ye meek of the earth, which have wrought his judgment; **seek righteousness, seek meekness**: it may be ye shall be hid in the day of the LORD's anger.
KJV

God had Israel create another Sacred Place where He would dwell, and men could come before Him. It started with the Tabernacle, which resided at Shiloh. Then His Holy Space was transferred to the temple built by Solomon in Jerusalem. The temple also required those who were in it to be in a purified state of holiness. When they went to the temple to seek God, they could not go just any way they wanted to. **When we meet God, it is on His terms, not ours.**

In the Old Testament, the High Priest would enter into the most holy place in the temple once a year to meet with God. There were specific details given to the High Priest, by God, on how he was to proceed with his duties. When it came to the rituals for the most holy place, the priest's life was dependent upon him following God's instructions on how he should enter that Holy Space where God resided. He would be entering God's presence and if he did it the wrong way, he could lose his life. They would tie ropes around the High Priest and put bells around his ankles. If the priest entered into God's presence with sin, or not following God's direct instructions, he would drop dead. If the priests outside did not hear the bells ringing on the High Priest's ankles, then that would indicate he was dead, and they would pull him out. God was serious about how they approached Him.

In the book of Exodus, God told Moses that the ground he was standing on was Holy Ground. The ground was not holy in itself but became holy because of the presence of God. When Moses came to the burning bush, God told him to take off his sandals because he was walking on Holy Ground. Moses complied and showed reverence towards God. He was required to follow the instructions of God to enter into God's Holy Space (remove shoes), and submission to God was also required to stay in that Sacred Place that became sacred because of God's presence.

When the 70 leaders of the tribe of Israel had to come to the mount of God (Exodus), they had to purify themselves before they came before God. Examples are all over scripture showing reverence to God when we seek to enter into His presence (Holy Space). Why would we think that it would be any different when we come before Him in prayer?

Why is it that so many Christians have unanswered prayers? One reason is they are not seeking God at His temple! Some do not even know what the temple is. Solomon understood that the temple he built was not the real temple of God but just a place that God would put His presence (Holy Space) for a short time to dwell with men. Pay attention to what Solomon is revealing in these verses:

2 Chron 6:18-21
18 "But will God indeed dwell with men on the earth? Behold, heaven and the heaven of heavens cannot contain You. **How much less this temple which I have built!** 19 Yet regard the prayer of Your servant and his supplication, O LORD my God, and listen to the cry and the prayer which Your servant is praying before You: 20 that Your eyes may be open toward this temple day and night, toward the place where You said You would put Your name, that You may hear the prayer which Your servant makes toward this place. 21 And may You hear the supplications of Your servant and of Your people Israel, when they pray toward this place. Hear from heaven Your dwelling place, and when You hear, forgive.
NKJV

Solomon knew that the temple he built was not the real temple and just stood as a replica. He was aware that nothing could be constructed by man to contain God. Yet God, in His love and mercy, gave to us something greater than anything man could build. There is a more magnificent temple, and Christ revealed this to us.

Matt 12:5-6
5 Or have ye not read in the law, how that on the sabbath days the priests in the temple profane the sabbath, and are blameless?
6 But I say unto you, **That in this place is one greater than the temple.**
KJV

Christ is the head of the Body of Christ, and all that believe (have God's Spirit) and obey Christ are members of this body. This body is God's temple on the earth. To seek His face, you must enter the temple of God. Please read carefully:

John 2:19
19 Jesus answered and said unto them, destroy this temple, and **in three days I will raise it up.**
KJV

Christ was speaking of His body, and when He raised it up, He raised up all those IN CHRIST with Him. To be in Christ is to be a person that believes in who He is and what He says. Christ said **we must be hearers of the Word plus doers and this confirms that we truly believe.**

Eph 2:20-22
20 And are built upon the foundation of the apostles and prophets, Jesus Christ himself being the chief corner stone;
21 In whom all the building fitly framed together groweth unto an holy temple in the Lord:
22 **In whom ye also are builded together for an habitation of God through the Spirit.**
KJV

Christ's death and resurrection has granted us access to God's presence in a deeper and spiritual way. However, what we have to ask ourselves is, "Does His sacrifice, give us the right to approach God any way we want?" Christ commanded that we pray to the Father in His name. Christ is our spiritual High Priest (in heaven). Just as the high priest of the earthly temple was the only one who had access to the Holy of Holies on earth, the High Priest in heaven is the only one who has access to the throne room in the real temple in the third heaven. This is the reason Christ said the only way to the Father is through Him. The reason we MUST pray to the Father in Christ's name (Jesus/Yehoshua), as I stated earlier, is because He is the High Priest and He has access to God's throne.

The worldly churches have been teaching that there is nothing else required to abide in that Sacred Place, which is IN CHRIST. God has shown us that there certainly are requirements to maintain our position in this Sacred Place. Someone is lying, and it sure is not God! To access the Holy Space, we must abide in the Sacred Place, which is the Body of Christ. Christ emphasizes this, but many miss it.

John 15:7-8
7 **If ye abide** in me, and my words abide in you, **ye shall ask what ye will, and it shall be done unto you.**
8 Herein is my Father glorified, that ye bear much fruit; so shall ye be my disciples.
KJV

This is a very powerful promise, and I need you to pay careful attention. We must abide in Christ, who is the spiritual temple and that Sacred Place. To do this, we must ensure that Christ's words abide in us, which means we must continue in His words, **which is simply to obey them.** Then **whatever we ask will be done (according to God's will) because to be in Christ by obeying Him gives us access to the Holy Space of God.** When we have access to that Holy Space, anything we ask (pray) that is in line with His promises, **He will do. God does not lie!** So why are the requests that you are asking God according to His will, through proper prayer, not being answered in your life? If you are not in Christ, which is to obey Him, then none of the promises for those in Christ are for you. Some of you have been lied to! No promise will manifest in your life if you are not obeying Christ. This is the actual reason why so many prayers go unanswered.

Poisoned

The devil's devices keep you dependent on what cannot help you. The world pumps poisons into you through the air, processed food, contaminated water, and other devices. These poisons make you sick. Then they hide any knowledge of natural things that can heal you so you cannot be cured. Then they provide you with medications that cannot cure but takes away the symptoms or allows you to bear them. You become dependent on this false medication that is not an antidote, and they keep you in this state and feed off you (monetarily). Like a drug dealer, they want you hooked on their drugs so the money keeps rolling in. So you wonder, what does this have to do with prayer?

See, unscrupulous ministers (not all) tell you because of grace, you can sin all you want and have no worries because you cannot lose your salvation. This allows you to be saturated with sin. You become spiritually sick and it will manifest throughout your life. They hide the fact that walking in obedience to Christ is the cure for your sickness. In addition, since there is no obedience, your prayers go unanswered. You have no access to God because your sin separates you from Him. They then use parlor tricks, grand lying speeches, and demonic activity to fool you into thinking they are your way to answered prayers (at a cost).

I recently heard one of these false prophets state, "You don't need to pray." His answer for your troubles is to plant a seed (money). Through hype, emotionally-charged messages, gimmicks, and psychology, they keep you coming to them for access to God, which in truth they do not have. Entertainment, sweet words that provide no sustenance, witchcraft disguised as gifts, and false anointing are used to dull your symptoms. This is the medication that does not cure, but like addicts, you keep going back to the drug dealer to get more to hide the symptoms. This is why it is so important to learn the proper way to pray and the requirements for our prayers to be heard.

Chapter 3

God's Holy Space

People have said that God comes out of eternity to meet us in time, but this is not correct. Wherever God's presence is located, the area becomes a Holy Space. A Holy Space cannot reside in time, it is always in eternity. Many believers can testify that they have been in a place where God's presence was so strong that it seemed that time stopped. What is so sad is that the high majority of those who profess to be Christians have never experienced this. It is not because it's not available to them but because they have never been taught how to enter into God's Holy Space.

The first time I experienced this was when I received the sanctification. Let me share this testimony. I remember Mrs. McIntyre opening the door shortly after I knocked on it. What I wasn't prepared for was the shocking look on her face as if she saw a ghost. In actuality it turned out she did, and this Ghost was Holy. While standing in the doorway, she immediately said, "You have to go to church with us tomorrow." I told her I was going to church, but had made plans to visit a church with a friend. She told me to just make sure I was in church. When I asked her why, she said, "I can see the Holy Ghost all over you and something is about to happen, so you need to be in church." **This should be a wake-up call for those who think they do not have to attend a church**. God can fellowship with us anywhere, but there is a reason Scripture says that we should not forsake the gathering of the saints.

Mother McIntyre invited me in, and she, her daughter Linda, and I enjoyed fellowship through the evening. These are the two Christians that I credit with me accepting (early in my Christian walk) the knowledge of walking in holiness. Mother McIntyre was an older woman wearing glasses with a warm smile who had this outpouring of pleasantness about her. Five minutes after you meet her, you know she is a Christian that truly walks with God. To this day, I have not met a Christian who I think more highly of than this saint. I thank God that He put such good role models as Linda and Mother McIntyre in my life when I was a young Christian. When you observe people walking in holiness, it is encouragement that you can also.

I was curious about what she said because I did not feel anything, which is normal for those who have not received the Holy Spirit as of yet. I was a new Christian convert with only head knowledge. God had been showing me things, but I had little understanding of what they were. I thought I knew the Bible pretty well, but now as a seasoned teacher of the Word, I look back at what I knew then and just laugh. It was late when I left, and I drove home and went to bed. When I awoke the next morning, I had no recollection of what Mother McIntyre said to me.

A friend and I met at an old warehouse-looking building that was converted into a church. I don't remember the name of the church, but I know "last day deliverance" was part of it. I will never forget that day. I don't remember what the message was, but the pastor made an altar call for those who wanted to be saved or needed prayer. I went up for prayer and I remember being the second person from the left end of the altar. The altar was a group of three or four steps that led up to the platform from which the pastor was preaching. There were approximately forty people up at the altar.

When he started praying for us, he came to my side of the platform to lay hands on those he would pray for. I was the second person. I don't even remember what he said! He placed his hand on my stomach and prayed, and I started feeling a vibration that started in my feet. It slowly began to work its way up my body, and it felt like every molecule in me was on the verge of exploding. It was not painful, just powerful. I remember when it hit my hands that they started shaking violently. Picture a firefighter's hose with no one holding it and the nozzle swinging back and forth wildly. This was what was happening to my hands, just a lot faster. Then I screamed, but not from pain. The scream just came and continued for what I thought was about one or two minutes. I remember turning to run, but there was a potted plant next to me by the altar. The plant was blocking the direction that I planned on running in. I doubt I would have been able to run anyhow. I closed my eyes and continued screaming, and then it was over.

When I looked up the pastor was looking at me as if I needed to hurry up, which I thought was surprising because there must have been at least thirty-five more people he needed to pray for, so why was he hurrying me? I turned and looked beside me and was in total shock. The altar was empty. Remember, there were about forty people up there and he was praying individually for all of us. He prayed for me second so after me he prayed for thirty-eight more people, finished, and they all had taken their seats. I could not believe it.

I turned around and quickly walked back to my seat, but as I glanced up, I realized I had been standing up there for more than forty-five minutes. If you would have told me that before I noticed all the people were seated and the time on the clock, I would have said that you were lying. I had no idea what had happened. When I sat down, my friend said something to the effect that people were looking at their watches saying, "Will he hurry up so we can go?" As the pastor said the benediction and closed the service, we exited the building, and something else peculiar happened.

I started noticing that every car passing by was brand new. I thought that was strange, but as I looked closer, I realized that even the old cars looked brand new. I looked around, and everything was bright. I mean everything I looked at, had bright shining colors. It was as if the whole world just got a brand new paint job. Or as if I had been looking at the world with dark shades on and God had removed them. Later on, in my spiritual walk, I understood that it was not the world that had changed, it was me. God had removed the shadow of death that resides on all unbelievers. He sanctified me (set me apart).

Acts 26:18
18 To open their eyes, and to turn them from darkness to light, and from the power of Satan unto God, that they may receive forgiveness of sins, and inheritance among them which are sanctified by faith that is in me.
KJV

Glory be to God for the great things He has done, for He so loved the world that He gave us His only Son, to die in our place and turn us back to the Father that we might be part of His Holy Kingdom. Hallelujah!

Over the years I have witnessed and heard testimonies from others believers, which are similar to mine. I have also experienced deliverance when going through struggles in my walk and encountered the same happenings, but not of the same magnitude. God has also used me to do deliverance on others where they have testified that after the prayer the room got bright.

What I want to emphasize is the time stoppage. Remember I said earlier that God comes and meets with us. Many have taught that He comes out of eternity to meet us in time, but this is not accurate. God does not exist in time. Time cannot exist where God is because His essence is eternity. When we meet with Him, we come out of time and meet Him in eternity. Isn't it funny how this lines up with what scientists say would happen if a man could travel the speed of light? They have concluded that time would slow for the person moving at this speed but back here on earth, time would be moving at a normal pace. When the person returned to earth, very little time would have gone by for them, but on earth, everyone would be much older. **Time keeps on moving but eternity does not move.** Therefore, when we meet with God, what seems like no time at all in His presence can be hours in time. Time is warped around us who are in God's presence. Moses did not get old even though he aged. He is the man in the Bible that spent the most time in that Holy Space communing with God. The time went by, but his body did not decay at a normal rate. He lived to 120 years but could have lived longer because his eyes were not dim and his natural strength had not diminished. Joshua lived to a hundred and ten, and Kaleb was a young man when he was old. These are the three who spent the most time with God when He journeyed with Israel from Egypt to the Promised Land. The Israelites' clothes and shoes did not wear out, a benefit of spending time in God's presence. **There is no decay in eternity; decay is death, and death only exists in time.**

Every Christian that is praying correctly will experience a time when they feel that connection to God in their prayers, and it feels like a shift in time. When the prayer is done, you will notice that a lot of time went by yet it felt like the prayer was not as long as the time. It is also true that many Christians have felt this even when they were praying wrong because God will often look past our ignorance through His mercy. What I am about to reveal to you through the Word of God is the correct way of praying, which will increase the time you spend in that Holy Time of communion with God. It will also enable young (spiritually) believers to learn the correct way according to scriptures, which will give them a head start in their relationship with God.

Chapter 4

Correct Prayer

Why do people pray with their palms together? Do you even know? Would you be surprised to know that this goes against the directions we have from the Word of God? Nowhere in scripture are believers or anyone else described as praying with palms together. The Bible teaches that we are to lift up our hands and spread them towards heaven when we pray.

1 Tim 2:8
8 I will therefore that men pray every where, **lifting up holy hands**, without wrath and doubting.
KJV

Isa 1:15
15 And **when ye spread forth your hands**, I will hide mine eyes from you: yea, when ye make many prayers, I will not hear: your hands are full of blood.
KJV

Ps 28:2
2 Hear the voice of my supplications, when I cry unto thee, **when I lift up my hands toward thy holy oracle.**
KJV

Ps 63:4
4 Thus will I bless thee while I live: **I will lift up my hands in thy name.**
KJV

Ps 88:9
9 Mine eye mourneth by reason of affliction: LORD, I have called daily upon thee, **I have stretched out my hands unto thee.**
KJV

Ps 141:2
2 Let my prayer be set forth before thee as incense; and **the lifting up of my hands as the evening sacrifice.**
KJV

I especially like this one:

Lam 2:19
19 Arise, cry out in the night: in the beginning of the watches pour out thine heart like water before the face of the Lord: **lift up thy hands toward him for the life of thy young children, that faint for hunger in the top of every street.**
KJV

Closed Palms

If the examples from the scriptures are arms uplifted, then where do the closed palms come from? While studying different Eastern religions for my degree in religious studies, I found that their practice is to pray with palms together to focus the energy that leaves the hands back into the body. It is a way of self-empowerment, but it is false. It teaches a person to depend on self and not on an outside force. The truth is, self cannot save you. **When death comes for you, self will have no answer.**

These are the moments when I wish I could show you what I have seen in the spirit realm. When Christ says we are the light of the world, He is not lying. I remember praying and asking God to show me how He saw me. I thought I was doing so well in my walk IN Christ and wanted God's approval. So I asked Him to show me what He sees when He looks at me. After He showed me, I cried on and off for about two weeks every time I pictured how He saw me.

In a vision, God showed me crying out to Him. I was standing with my arms reaching up to God. I had beams of white light bursting out of my palms and my mouth. Nevertheless, what was so disturbing was that my body was covered in a black tar like substance from head to toe. The tar looked disgusting. I received the revelation that the white light bursting out of me represented the Holy Spirit in me, but the black tar was the filth of the flesh. It was beautiful to see what God had deposited in me. However, the recognition of the filth of the flesh left me tearful. I was humbled and had a better understanding of the saying that our righteousness is as filthy rags in the sight of God. I was filthy!

For young Christians, the truth of who we are before God can be a hard pill to swallow. **The truth will allow us to overcome all the challenges in our Christian walk.** I also learned a lot about the things going on in the spirit realm that are hidden from our natural eyes. I often pray for people, and they tell me they feel heat in the area where my hands contact their bodies. Therefore the beam of light I was shown was the power of God flowing through my hands. As I reflected back on what I was shown, I began to realize that many times I would cry out to God and my hands would rise up. As a young Christian, I thought a lot about this, but I was about to experience something so powerful that it would lead me to search the scriptures for answers on how we should pray.

I was still a young Christian going through spiritual growth, which comes with trials and tribulations. God was in the process of purifying my soul, and it was a hard process. I do not remember what the situation was back then, but I was lamenting over something God was taking me through. I cried myself to sleep and went into a vision while sleeping. When I say "vision" I mean it was a dream so vivid and clear that it went beyond any ordinary dream and was a message from God. In the dream, two men came over to me and lifted my hands. They pointed to the corner of the bed where I usually kneel and pray. As I got off the bed and kneeled down into my prayer position, they once again raised up both of my hands. I came out of the vision.

I knew God was telling me to pray, but could not understand why I was being told to hold up my arms. I got down and prayed, which was more like crying out to God. When I finished praying, I felt a release. As I got up, I noticed two white feathers were lying on the floor by my bed. I was perplexed because I could not understand where they came from. I knew I had a pillow with feathers inside, but there was no hole in it. I asked myself, "Is God letting me know that there were two angels sent to bring me through this difficult period in my life?" I came to the conclusion that God was revealing to me that His angels were watching over me according to His Word. But then I had the problem of understanding why they lifted up my arms.

Anytime I have a question about my Christian walk and the things that God is showing me, I go to the scriptures for answers. I started searching the scriptures to find people praying with their hands/arms uplifted. I was shocked to find it was all over the Bible. Then I read Paul's instructions on praying with hands uplifted. I saw where Solomon knelt with arms spread to the heavens. I read of people praising in the temple with arms uplifted. I started realizing it was the norm, and it was all over the scriptures.

2 Chron 6:13
13 For Solomon had made a brasen scaffold, of five cubits long, and five cubits broad, and three cubits high, and had set it in the midst of the court: and upon it he stood, **and kneeled down upon his knees**

before all the congregation of Israel, and spread forth his hands toward heaven,
KJV

Psalms
Ps 143:6
6 **I stretch forth my hands unto thee**: my soul thirsteth after thee, as a thirsty land. Selah.
KJV

Ezra 9:5
5 And at the evening sacrifice I arose up from my heaviness; and having rent my garment and my mantle, **I fell upon my knees, and spread out my hands unto the LORD my God.**
KJV

Job 11:13
13 If thou **prepare thine heart, and stretch out thine hands toward him;**
KJV

So why is this not being taught in the churches? I know many will say it does not matter, but it does, otherwise the angels in the vision would not have lifted up my hands. I then started remembering the verses in Exodus 17 where Moses was watching over the battle between Israel and their enemies and when he lifted up his hands Israel would be prevailing, but when he lowered his hands, the enemy started prevailing. Aaron and Hur then came and propped up his hands, and Israel won the battle. **Everything God puts in the scriptures is a message for the everyday believer.** It is not a coincidence that the chapter before 17 (Ex 16) is where Israel first gets manna from heaven. God then leads them out of the wilderness of Sin (first part of chapter 17) and Moses strikes the rock of Horeb, which then pours out water for the people to drink.

In the same manner when we accept Christ as the true bread from heaven (Word of God), He then leads us out of sin, and we receive the living water from our rock, which is Christ. The living waters represent the Holy Spirit that is poured into us, and we become springs of living water.

John 7:38-39

38 He that believeth on me, as the scripture hath said, out of his belly shall flow rivers of living water .

39(But **this spake he of the Spirit, which they that believe on him should receive**: for the Holy Ghost was not yet given; because that Jesus was not yet glorified.)

KJV

They received the water that poured out of a rock, which foreshadowed the real living waters (Holy Spirit) that we as believers all receive. What is the first lesson Israel learned after receiving their water? **You win battles against the enemy by lifting your hands to heaven. We win spiritual battles by knowing how to pray.** That is the revelation of why Moses had to lift up his hands to win the battle against the Amalekites. The Amalekites were the giants of the Old Testament, and they represent the giants in our lives that fight against us. Please take note again that when his hands went down, they would start losing the battle. The arms uplifted have to mean and accomplish something. **When we lift and stretch our arms and hands to God, we are showing dependency on Him.** When a small child lifts up his hands to a parent, he is showing he wants to be lifted up into the parent's presence. With God, we are acknowledging that He is our helper in our time of need. That is why Paul instructed that we pray with arms uplifted. That is why all those great men of the Bible prayed with arms uplifted. They lifted up their arms to enter God's presence, and bring Him into the battle. It shows we are agreeing to His terms according to the example left us in scripture. When we pray according to tradition or self and not according to scripture, God is in no way obligated to answer.

When we pray with palms turned in and held together, we are unknowingly portraying a closed system of inner dependency. It is a symbol of self and shows we are our own gods. This is the ideology taught in many pagan beliefs of the personal god of self within us. It is not by chance that this way of praying has been syncretized into the Christian church. It is a direct contradiction to what is taught in the Bible. Are we going to teach our children the example held in scripture that has been practiced by so many men of God? Or are we going to adapt to a worldly example that symbolically denies our reliance on God? God told Moses to take off his shoes because he was on Holy Ground. What do you think would have happened if he said, "Sorry, but I would rather keep them on?" Remember when we meet God it is on His terms, not ours. If you truly want to meet with Him, please follow scriptural instructions!

I know many of you will say that you have been praying for years and have received answers, so nothing is wrong with the way that you pray. I want you to remember that many men of God did things the wrong way when they were afar off from God. When God starts the process of drawing us closer to Him, just as with Israel, He corrects us on the proper way to do things so we can enter His presence. This is not about doing what we want to do or maintaining traditions that come from men, and not God. This is about utilizing the access we have in Christ to enter into that Holy Space of God's presence.

I have received numerous testimonies from believers that have embraced the biblical teaching on prayer. They testify of experiencing a spiritual opening above their heads during prayer. I have also experienced this while praying. It is as if a portal opens up between us and God. We receive from Him a downloading of His power to be vessels to bring about change in others and our own lives. To enter God's presence, we have to come according to His terms. We can continue to do things our way and limit our relationship with God, or we can say, "Father, not my will, but let Your will be done." We can come up to a new height in our relationship with God. We have the access, and it is our decision if we use it or not.

We can stand in the outer court of the temple watching those who are hungry and thirsty for a deeper relationship with God. They will be passing by as they enter into the inner court headed to the Holy of Holies. On the other hand, we can come to the realization that our destiny is embedded in Christ and we have to walk as He walked. Christ's steps took Him to the inner court of the temple, then to the Holy Place, and finally into the Holy of Holies where He entered eternity in the presence of the Father. All those who walk with Him will stand before the Father with Him. **Just remember, when we meet God it will be on His terms, not ours!**

Knees Bowed

A friend requested that I minister to a young man that had been going through deep struggles with sins that had crept into his life from some family problems. I could tell from our conversations that he wanted to be delivered, and he was actively seeking after God. We were speaking on the phone, and I was taking him through scriptures. I was addressing his struggles and showing him from the Word of God the solutions to his problems. After I finished ministering to him, I asked if I could pray with him, and he said, "Yes." I started praying and was surprised when the Holy Spirit spoke to me, and advised me that the young man was not active in the prayer. I stopped praying and asked the young man what he was doing, and he said he was lying on his bed in prayer with me. I told him to get off his bed and bow down before God, which he did, and then I continued the prayer. After we were done, I contemplated the message in what took place. **God was not accepting the prayer because the young man was not showing any reverence to God.** How many times have we been too lazy to get out of bed and show reverence to God in prayer?

I have learned over the years that if I get a spiritual attack while sleeping and wake up to go into prayer while still lying on the bed, my prayer is not answered. The spiritual attack will continue. However, when I get out of bed and pray to God bowed down with hands uplifted, the attack stops. Many people who have unanswered prayers do not even realize it is because they are not praying according to the examples given to us in scripture. When we line up with the examples God left us and show reverence in our prayers, then our petitions are heard by God. He will answer us in one way or another. When we do it according to what we believe, which does not line up with scripture, there is no assurance that the prayer will be answered. The enemy can then utilize the opportunity to come and interject a false answer, but the situation we are praying about is never resolved.

There are other facets to assure our prayers are heard, but we are required to show submission and reliance by how we position our bodies as an act of reverence to God. Let me add for the naysayers who would like to question saying, "What about the times we are unable to kneel or stretch forth our hands?" God knows what is going on. If you are about to have a car accident and you cry out to God for protection, He will not reject your prayer because you are not kneeling with hands uplifted. **We serve an understanding God.** Nevertheless, when we are able, let us pray in the right manner to assure we are granted our petitions. Let us also give God the respect and reverence He deserves.

Heads Bowed
(real worship)

I want to touch base on a big misconception about worship. I often go to churches and hear worship leaders announce that it is time to worship. I then watch as the congregation stand on their feet and sing songs of praise, jump, shout, and do everything except worship. What is worship? Worship is to bow your body and or head before the Lord and glorify Him.

Ex 34:6-8
6 And the LORD passed by before him, and proclaimed, The LORD, The LORD God, merciful and gracious, longsuffering, and abundant in goodness and truth,
7 Keeping mercy for thousands, forgiving iniquity and transgression and sin, and that will by no means clear the guilty; visiting the iniquity of the fathers upon the children, and upon the children's children, unto the third and to the fourth generation.
8 And Moses made haste, **and bowed his head toward the earth, and worshipped.**
KJV

Ex 4:31
31 And the people believed: and when they heard that the LORD had visited the children of Israel, and that he had looked upon their affliction, then **they bowed their heads and worshipped.**
KJV

2 Chron 20:18
18 And **Jehoshaphat bowed his head with his face to the ground: and all Judah and the inhabitants of Jerusalem fell before the LORD, worshipping the LORD.** (KJV)

Ps 95:6
6 O come, **let us worship and bow down: let us kneel before the LORD our maker.**
KJV

When we start our prayer, the first step is to bow our heads, and glorify God. If you are not bowed, then you are not worshipping. We bow as a form of submission and reverence, and then we give glory to God. When Christ taught the disciples how to pray, he starts the prayer with worship.

Matt 6:9
9 After this manner therefore pray ye: Our Father which art in heaven, **Hallowed be thy name.**
KJV

The Deception in Incorrect Prayer

Something that I think we have gotten away from in the Christians churches of today is training up believers on the devices of the enemy. With the prevalence of a watered down Gospel more focused on the blessings than on the foundational teachings of the Apostles, it seems we have lost the knowledge of how the enemy attacks the church. The Devil's devices were taught to the church by the disciples so they were prepared to defend themselves against the tricks and traps that the enemy used against them.

2 Cor 2:11
11 Lest Satan should get an advantage of us: **for we are not ignorant of his devices.**
KJV

In warfare, one of the most effective devices is to disrupt the communication between the soldiers in battle and the headquarters. If you can stop the lines of communication then you gain a significant advantage over the enemy.

Satan's kingdom has done a good job of hindering the believers' prayers by putting forth images and traditions that violate what the Bible teaches on prayer. Let me reiterate an earlier point.

God answers our prayers because of His mercy, He is not obligated to if we are praying incorrectly. The Kingdom of Satan understands this and has taken measures to reinforce these incorrect ways of praying to hinder our prayers. However, when we pray according to scripture, God is **obligated** to answer us.

One Hand Raised

I have seen many beautiful pictures making their way around the internet of people in beautiful sceneries praying. When believers see these images, they want to reenact them or mimic the positions shown. The only problem is there are diabolical deceptions in these pictures. Have you seen the one where there is a silhouette of a person with one hand raised to the sky and the other hand facing down to the ground? It is a breathtaking scene but the only problem is, it represents the occult. There is a saying among occultists taken from an ancient pagan philosopher named Hermes Trismegistus. The saying is, "So it is above so it is below." You will find this saying in many areas of witchcraft and sorcery. They even incorporate it into their spells. The saying is also symbolized by one arm raised towards the sky with the other pointed towards the ground. This positioning of the body is very demonic.

Where in scripture does it say to pray with one hand towards heaven? There are absolutely no examples in scripture of anyone praying in this manner. Nowhere in scripture does it say for us to pray in this manner. Yet, if you go on the internet right now and search for images depicting prayer, you will see that this prayer position is common. We can be so easily deceived when ignorant of scripture.

One knee bowed

Isa 45:23-24
23 I have sworn by myself, the word is gone out of my mouth in righteousness, and shall not return, That unto me every knee shall bow, every tongue shall swear.
24 Surely, shall one say, in the LORD have I righteousness and strength: even to him shall men come; and all that are incensed against him shall be ashamed.
KJV

The scripture speaks of everyone being before God and every knee will be bowed. So where does the one knee prayer come from? The term "genuflection" means a person bowing one knee in a sit-squat position. It is used in many Protestant denominations and the Catholic Church to show reverence or respect to the sacraments. We have already seen the examples from scripture of bowing the knees in worship and praying with both knees bowed. If scripture shows that God desires both knees bowed in prayer and in worship, then why would we as Christians adopt a one-knee position against the Word of God? Does what the Bible say really matter or are we allowed to do whatever we please?

Facing the sun

Ezek 8:16-17
16 And he brought me into the inner court of the LORD's house, and, behold, at the door of the temple of the LORD, between the porch and the altar, were about five and twenty men, with their backs toward the temple of the LORD, and **their faces toward the east; and they worshipped the sun toward the east.**
17 Then he said unto me, Hast thou seen this, O son of man? Is it a light thing to the house of Judah that they commit the abominations which they commit here? for they have filled the land with violence, and have returned to provoke me to anger: and, lo, they put the branch to their nose.
KJV

Have you noticed that many of the depictions of people praying today have them facing the sun as if they are praying to it as a symbol of God? Do you realize that sun worship was forbidden in scripture and we should avoid any appearance of doing this? Some might see nothing wrong with this if the person is truly praying to God but we must always be wary of our actions being misconstrued to support something that is against God.

In scripture, the Israelites were told to pray with their faces toward the temple where God resided in the Holy of Holies. Depending on where you lived in Israel, you could be facing any direction. They did not pray towards the east unless the temple was in that direction from where they lived. In addition, they definitely did not pray towards the rising sun because they knew this was the creation and not the Creator.

When God took Ezekiel to the temple in a vision and showed him what the people were doing, the greatest abomination that God pointed out were the elders of Israel praying facing the east towards the sun. God called this an abomination.

The book of Job points out the severity of the sin in giving any type of worship or praise to any heavenly body.

Job 31:26-28
26 If I beheld the sun when it shined, or the moon walking in brightness;
27 And my heart hath been secretly enticed, or my mouth hath kissed my hand:
28 This also were an iniquity to be punished by the judge: **for I should have denied the God that is above.**
KJV

Even though many people are ignorant to what Job pointed out, the devil is not and will use anything we do in ignorance as a way to accuse us before God. We must understand that our actions, even when innocent, can be a hindrance to others who might see us as giving approval to something that is wrong in the eyes of God. This is why God emphasizes in many places in the Bible that we are to do exactly what is given in scripture when it comes to the things of God. We are not to take away from nor add to these things.

The Devil wants us to deviate just a little from the straight and narrow knowing that as we continue down the way in the end we'll find ourselves way off the mark and will be wondering how we got there. If the instructions say, "Go west," and we start walking southwest, we will barely notice the difference after taking a couple steps. It will seem as if we are right there. However, a few miles down the line if we turn to see where the others are that have followed the instructions completely, we will not even be able to see them. We will realize that we are the lost sheep who are lost in the wilderness and the wolves will be on our tracks howling. **Follow God's Biblical instructions as if your life depends on it because in truth, your eternal life does. Stay on track.**

Chapter 5

Positioning Our Hearts
(So Our Prayers are Answered)

No unconfessed sin

There is a reason that Christ instructed the believers to ask for forgiveness before they made their petition to God in prayer. The Bible speaks about sin causing a separation between us and God. **We are not IN Christ when we are IN sin!** Like the high priest that walks into the Holy of Holies with sin, even though we are not killed, we are rejected. We have no right to petition God for anything other than forgiveness. **Confessing our sins before God and repenting (turning) from the sin brings us back into Christ and we recover our access into the Holy of Holies.**6 Before we can petition God, we **must** confess our sins. Please do not forget that repentance must follow confession.

Ps 66:18-20
18 If I regard iniquity in my heart, the Lord will not hear me:
19 But verily God hath heard me; he hath attended to the voice of my prayer.
20 Blessed be God, which hath not turned away my prayer, nor his mercy from me.
KJV

If we have unconfessed sin, God will not hear our prayers that do not come with repentance. In addition, when we reject the commandments given to us through Christ by refusing to walk in them, our prayers become an abomination to God. This is the reason so many Christians, when speaking honestly, will admit that God is not answering their prayers. They hear their brothers and sisters speaking of how God has answered prayers, and secretly they are reasoning within themselves why their prayers are not being answered. A person that is dishonest with themselves will never grow spiritually. You have to face the truth to correct the mistakes in your spiritual life. God answers the prayers of His children, and when I line up with His Word on prayer, He answers all my petitions. Yes, no, or wait, but He answers.

Prov 28:9
9 He that turneth away his ear from hearing the law, even his prayer shall be abomination.
KJV

Unforgiveness and Prayer

I could write volumes on the subject of unforgiveness. It is one of the most dangerous sins and the one, which can easily go unnoticed. **This is an issue, which we have to teach children about from an early age.** In truth, forgiveness is part of the foundation of our salvation. Without forgiveness, all of us would have been doomed. We just spoke about the necessity of having no unconfessed sin so our prayers can be answered.

When we are in sin, the only prayer God will hear from us is one that addresses our sin, before our petition. This brings us to the issue of unforgiveness. **If we do not forgive others according to the scriptural teaching on forgiving, then our sins will not be forgiven us.** If we are still in sin, then our prayers are an abomination before God. Unforgiveness causes a downward spiral into the abyss. I want to share a testimony with you about the dangers of unforgiveness.

Many years ago, I was speaking with a coworker and sharing with her the things of God. During our conversation, she shared with me that she had confessed Christ, but it was hard to forgive her mother for the trauma she went through as a child. Her mother was addicted to crack cocaine and was never a real mother to her and her siblings. She was the oldest and had to take on the position as mother to her little sisters and brother. She said she blamed her mother for stealing her childhood. Her mother was never around, and when she did come home, she would be in the company of some of the most ungodly people who traumatized her and her siblings. She explained how she hated her mother for years, and it was hard to release the hatred. Her story was so sad.

I, in turn, shared with her details from my life, and how I was mistreated by family members. Many of the events of my childhood were extremely painful. At the age of 27, I discovered that my father was not really my biological father. I went on to explain the circumstances that led to me finding my real father and the hardships I went through before and after that. I was actually attempting to comfort her by showing that she was not alone in having a harsh childhood. I also found it hard to forgive my parents, and it only came about after I confessed Christ and learned how to forgive.

I prayed with her, and that was the end of our conversation, but old memories were stirred up from our discussion. Weeks went by, and I went along with my regular routine. I began to notice that I felt weighted down in my spiritual life. I was also getting a lot of twitching on my body (book "Assault on Innocence" chapter 7). Every week I would have Bible study, but it was becoming a struggle to teach, which generally comes easily to me. I was struggling and could not put my finger on the problem.

One evening while I was at home I heard a knock on my door. It was a neighbor who was also one of my co-workers that I had just recently been ministering to about salvation. I was surprised to see him because although we were friendly to one another, he had seldom come to my door. Then he uttered the words that stopped me in my tracks. He said, "Williams, a voice spoke to me and told me to come and get you and take you out into the woods." Now you have to understand I am someone who believes the scripture that we cannot entirely trust anyone besides God. Therefore, I was thinking, "What in the world is going on, does he really think I am going to follow him out into the woods?" I replied, "What?" He repeated it to me and explained he didn't know who was speaking to him but he thought it might be God. I had to think on this one because to be honest, he was kind of scaring me. Reluctantly, I said, "ok."

Now at the time I was working at the state prison and living on the premises. The institution sat right in the Everglades of South Florida. Surrounding the institution were swamps and woods. The area he took me to was a wooded area that had just been through a forest fire. As we moved through the woods, you could smell the burnt wood in the air and the sound of crunching as we walked, stepping on burnt debris. I asked him if he knew where we were going, and he said, "No."

I started thinking maybe God just wanted me to continue ministering to him, so I started sharing the things of God. It was strange standing in the woods talking to him, looking around, and seeing all the trees burnt up. Then I felt saddened realizing this was just a waste to see all the trees black and charred. We finished talking and came to no certain conclusion, so we headed back out of the woods.

Right before we exited the woods, we walked into a circular clearing filled with the ashes of burned-up bushes.

I felt like I was in one of those Spike Lee movies where he would have the character spin around with the camera moving in a circular motion as the person's visual was spinning. As I walked around in the circular clearing, it hit me. I said to him, "This is judgment, God is about to bring judgment on someone." A split second later horror went through my soul as I realize the person was me.

Let me explain for those who do not understand how God communicates. Sometimes God will give you one word, but you will instantaneously be downloaded with a lot of information with the one word. At that moment, as I looked back at the burned up trees and scorched grounds of the woods, I knew exactly what I had done. I told my friend, "Thank you." I had to go and pray.

As I entered my apartment I got down on my knees, raised my hands up to the Lord, and began to repent for unforgiveness.

While I was ministering to the young lady and sharing all the things that had happened to me as a child, I started dwelling on those past hurts. As ministers, we have to sometimes share our past faults in the process of sharing the Gospel. When it is done correctly, it facilitates healing for others. Yet the emphasis has to be on healing and not our past hurts. I allowed feelings of unforgiveness back into my heart in remembering the things I went through. I had long ago forgiven my parents, but the conversation brought back those old feelings. Instead of rebuking those old feelings, I had secretly embraced them but with God, there are no secrets, even those we hide from ourselves.

Although we sin less and less as we mature into the image of Christ, we have to understand that it is a process that takes time. We speak guile, have sinful thoughts, and even sin in our actions as we go through the process of purification. **When we come to Christ, all our past/old sins are forgiven.** Many of the so-called gospels being preached in churches today do not explicitly teach the believers that sins we commit after our initial salvation must be confessed with a request from God for forgiveness. If this is not done, we are brought into judgment for the sin. As Christians, we are chastised by God for unconfessed sin.

Heb 12:10-14
10 For they verily for a few days chastened us after their own pleasure; but he for our profit, that we might be partakers of his holiness.
11 Now no chastening for the present seemeth to be joyous, but grievous: nevertheless afterward it yieldeth the peaceable fruit of righteousness unto them which are exercised thereby.
12 Wherefore lift up the hands which hang down, and the feeble knees;
13 And make straight paths for your feet, lest that which is lame be turned out of the way; but let it rather be healed.
14 Follow peace with all men, and holiness, without which no man shall see the Lord:
KJV

The privilege we have in our relationship with Christ is that we have access to God's mercy and forgiveness by Christ's

blood. Therefore, Christ becomes the doorway that we walk through to have access to the Father "to receive mercy and grace to help in the times of need." When we sin, we must ask for forgiveness and mercy. We are forgiven for our sin or receive mercy in God's chastisement of us. Here is the problem I had and the issue that makes unforgiveness such a serious sin.

Matt 6:15
15 But **if ye forgive not men their trespasses, neither will your Father forgive your trespasses.**
KJV

Every little (or big) sin I committed and then prayed for forgiveness was not being forgiven, because I was holding unforgiveness in my heart towards my parents who also were my brother and sister in Christ. **Do you realize that your post-baptism sins are forgiven on the condition that you also forgive others?**

Mark 11:25-26
25 And when ye stand praying, forgive, if ye have ought against any: that your Father also which is in heaven may forgive you your trespasses.
26 But **if ye do not forgive, neither will your Father which is in heaven forgive your trespasses.**
KJV

I want to add another gem of a revelation to what you have already learned on forgiveness/unforgiveness. Earlier in chapter one we talked about Christ's teaching on forgiving our brother seven times in a day. This teaching is mentioned in Luke 17:4 but I want to show you where it is expanded on.

Matt 18:21-22
21 Then came Peter to him, and said, Lord, **how oft shall my brother sin against me, and I forgive him? till seven times?**
22 Jesus saith unto him, I say not unto thee, Until seven times: but, Until seventy times seven.
KJV

Why did Christ say seven times seventy instead of just agreeing with Peter and confirming His teaching?

Christ had just finished expounding on what He wanted us to do concerning a brother that had sinned against us. He told the disciples that we should go to the person and discuss their fault. If he receives the correction, then forgive him. If he does not receive the correction, then take a witness and try again. If the person still does not receive the correction, then we are told to bring it before the church. If the person continues to not see their fault, then we are to treat them as an outcast. Jesus then reiterates the authority we have in the Body of Christ and when we gather together, He is with us.

It is shortly after this that Peter approaches the Messiah and asks Him the question of how many times we have to forgive a person. Here is the gem: Christ is about to rebuke Peter subtly and most scholars miss it. Peter was more concerned of when the forgiveness could end and he could use the authority as a member of the body to chastise his brother. Jesus does not confirm the seven times, which is the teaching He gave, as Peter well knew. Jesus speaks five words immediately to Peter that should have shaken his foundation. He said to Peter, "I say not unto thee." Jesus was speaking directly to Peter and indirectly to those with the same mindset as Peter. He is telling Peter that in his case, he needs to go beyond the teaching because of his shortcomings.

Matt 18:22
22 Jesus saith unto him, **I say not unto thee**, Until seven times: **but,** Until seventy times seven.
KJV

Christ knew Peter's heart and he also knew Peter's future. He knew Peter's past sins, which were cleansed by the Father. In addition, Peter still would need more forgiveness because he would soon deny Christ. Christ then explains the parable of the servant that owed his master millions and was forgiven only to turn and assault his fellow servant that owed him pennies. This was a direct warning to Peter and an indirect warning to us about forgiveness. Peter in the end would backslide and deny Christ and Christ would forgave him.

No one could ever need from Peter the amount of forgiveness that he would receive from God. Peter could not stop forgiving after seven times. He would have to allow them seventy times seven (490) because in the end He owe God so much. To whom much is given, much is required. Are you a Peter? I confess that I am.

Green Tree

A little while after I finished my prayer, I heard another knock on my door and it was my neighbor again. He explained that as he was walking along the road, something told him to look up at the big palm tree by the side of the road. He noticed how green and full it was and then he heard, "That's Samuel."

My petition was granted, repentance brought forgiveness, and I was back in right standing with God. So in comparison to the burnt up trees that we saw in the woods that symbolized judgment, forgiveness was symbolized by a green, healthy, and flourishing tree. **We must never forget that God is in control, and He determines our state according to our relationship in Christ.**

Ezek 17:24
24 And all the trees of the field shall know that I, the LORD, have brought down the high tree and exalted the low tree, dried up the green tree and made the dry tree flourish; I, the LORD, have spoken and have done it."
NKJV

God utilized this situation to not only teach me about unforgiveness but also to teach the young Christian brother that God does communicate with those seeking Him. This experience reinforced that God is real. The more we experience God, the harder it becomes for the enemy of our souls to turn us away from Him.

It is imperative that you understand this and that you teach this to others. Many times when you see Christians who seem to have no joy in their lives and look weighed down with a shadowy appearance, what you are seeing is the weight of sin on them. Many times, it is not because they are refusing to turn from sin but because they are holding unforgiveness and the end results can be seen in their lives. **Believe me: Unforgiveness has sent many a believer to hell.**

Matt 18:23-35
23 Therefore is the kingdom of heaven likened unto a certain king, which would take account of his servants.
24 And when he had begun to reckon, one was brought unto him, which owed him ten thousand talents.
25 But forasmuch as he had not to pay, his lord commanded him to be sold, and his wife, and children, and all that he had, and payment to be made.
26 The servant therefore fell down, and worshipped him, saying, Lord, have patience with me, and I will pay thee all.
27 Then the lord of that servant was moved with compassion, and loosed him, and forgave him the debt.
28 But the same servant went out, and found one of his fellowservants, which owed him an hundred pence: and he laid hands on him, and took him by the throat, saying, Pay me that thou owest.
29 And his fellowservant fell down at his feet, and besought him, saying, Have patience with me, and I will pay thee all.
30 And he would not: but went and cast him into prison, till he should pay the debt.
31 So when his fellowservants saw what was done, they were very sorry, and came and told unto their lord all that was done.
32 **Then his lord, after that he had called him, said unto him, O thou wicked servant, I forgave thee all that debt, because thou desiredst me:**
33 **Shouldest not thou also have had compassion on thy fellowservant, even as I had pity on thee?**
34 And his lord was wroth, and delivered him to the tormentors, till he should pay all that was due unto him.
35 So likewise shall my heavenly Father do also unto you, if ye from your hearts forgive not every one his brother their trespasses.
KJV

Understand that the servant owed the equivalent of a million dollars (approximately), and was forgiven yet was so cruel to his fellow servant who owed a lot less. What an enormous debt Christ paid with His life and blood to gain our eternal life. How trivial are the things we hold against our brothers and sisters pertaining to this life. **These are lessons we need to instill in babes in Christ because understanding this can be the difference between eternal life and hell.**

Chapter 6

This is Our Confidence

James 5:16-18

16 Confess your faults one to another, and pray one for another, that ye may be healed. The **effectual fervent** prayer of a **righteous** man availeth much.

17 Elias was a man **subject to like passions** as we are, and **he prayed earnestly** that it might not rain: and it rained not on the earth by the space of three years and six months.

18 And he prayed again, and the heaven gave rain, and the earth brought forth her fruit.

KJV

James is showing us as believers that Elias (Elijah) was a person just like us with like passions. Yet when he chose to walk righteously before God in an upright manner, it enabled the fervent prayers that he prayed to become effective and powerful. James is utilizing the truth in the testimony of scripture to encourage us that walking in righteousness and praying effectively will allow miracles to be manifested through us. **We can change the very environment around us by following the blueprint of God on prayer and walking in righteousness. This is a promise confirmed by Christ.**

John 15:7

7 If ye abide in me, and my words abide in you, **ye shall ask what ye will, and it shall be done unto you.**

KJV

Do you know that **IF** is a powerful word? If we abide in Christ, which is to walk according to His doctrine by keeping what He has commanded us, then we can ask the Father and He will grant it unto us. This is a promise from Christ. The key is to understand that the condition set by the word **IF** must be met to allow the promise to take affect. We must abide in Christ, which means to keep the commandments that He has left us.

John 15:10
10 If ye keep my commandments, ye shall abide in my love; even as I have kept my Father's commandments, and abide in his love.
KJV

If is indeed a powerful word. Our confidence is that God is a loving God and He knows our shortcomings and even our failures. **He is in this spiritual fight with us, fighting beside us and for us.** As we walk deeper into His love, He has left us the promise that what we ask from Him, He will do, and this again is our confidence.

1 John 3:22
22 And whatsoever we ask, we receive of him, because we keep his commandments, and do those things that are pleasing in his sight.
KJV

There are a lot of false doctrines circulating in many denominations, deceiving believers into embrace the lie that we can get everything we want from God without walking in obedience to His Word. Do not be deceived by the craftiness of the enemy and the false promises that come without condition.

God's promises are claimed by understanding and believing them. Faith in itself is believing in God's promises. Hence, if God gives us a promise that is backed up by Christ, granting our request if we meet certain conditions, then we must embrace in confidence this truth. We must not change it or rearrange it; we have to walk in it and receive the benefits of lining up with God's truth and not men's (or our own).

Our confidence is founded on the truth. If we position our bodies in reverence to God as demonstrated in the word of God with knees and head bowed, and arms uplifted, then we are praying according to God's Word.

Our confidence is established in the fact that we come before God with no sinful thoughts, unconfessed sins, or unforgiveness in our hearts. This enables our prayers because we have submitted our heart to God's will. When we are joyful in the truth of Christ's doctrine and we have embraced and established it in our lives because we love Him, then we are assured in confidence that we are granted an audience with the Father to hear our petitions.

When we come before the Father in the name of His Son with no vain requests or desires of the flesh but with spiritual desires that are guaranteed by the very promises of His Word, then this too is our confidence. We submit to His will and ask according to His will things for ourselves, for our brothers and sisters in Christ, and for those who are being called unto salvation to build up the Kingdom of God. We are then confident that our petition will be established by the power of the Almighty God.

1 John 5:14-15
14 And **this is the confidence that we have in him, that, if we ask any thing according to his will, he heareth us:**
15 And if **we know that he hear us, whatsoever we ask, we know that we have the petitions that we desired of him.**
KJV

The truth that the enemy of our souls does not want us to know is that God has proclaimed that He is obligated to answer all of the prayers that are prayed correctly by a child of God walking according to His will.

1 John 3:18-24
18 My little children, let us not love in word, neither in tongue; but in deed and in truth.
19 And hereby we know that we are of the truth, and shall assure our hearts before him.
20 For if our heart condemn us, God is greater than our heart, and knoweth all things.

21 Beloved, if our heart condemn us not, then have we confidence toward God.

22 And whatsoever we ask, we receive of him, **because** we **keep his commandments, and do those things that are pleasing in his sight.**

23 And this is his commandment, That we should believe on the name of his Son Jesus Christ, and love one another, as he gave us commandment.

24 And he that keepeth his commandments dwelleth in him, and he in him. And hereby we know that he abideth in us, by the Spirit which he hath given us.

KJV

Be Encouraged

One of the reasons I was inspired to write this book is because of the assault that I have witnessed coming against the prayer life of Christians. All over the media, I see those who are attacking prayer by using propaganda saying that prayer is a waste of time. It is almost comical that those who have no link to God, because of their wicked ways and their stance against everything that He has established, believe they can be a voice of reason on the benefits of prayer or lack thereof. Many Christians are being weakened by this assault because secretly they are wondering why their prayers are not being answered. The enemy will always give us an easy out by blaming God to convince us that He is not listening.

I remember watching a movie where the supposed hero was in dire straits surrounded by a pack of wolves and prayed to God but received no answer. He then blasphemed God with his words, then turned and said he would take care of the situation himself. The movie ended leaving the viewer with the false belief that the so-called hero would be able to defeat the pack of wolves by his own power, not needing God. **People today are so easily deceived by Hollywood. The reality is there would have been some well-fed wolves.** Hollywood is pushing the premise that people have god potential in themselves and do not need to pray to God but are gods in their own rights. Yet these same Hollywood stars are dying left and right, bound up in addictions, committing suicide, and being overcome by human situations. Just like the well-fed wolves, their lives are proof of where the real fairy tale is found.

I have seen people curse God on the news with contorted faces saying it is a waste of time to pray to Him because He has not answered anyone's prayers and it is all fairy tales. What does a sinner know about answered prayer? God will only hear a prayer of repentance from them before He hears anything else unless He bestows them with mercy. The haters of God cry out against Him and too many times Christians place themselves in situations to hear these cries and then begin to question their faith.

Do not fall for the deception. I have seen my prayers answered. God has instructed me to go and pray for a man about to be taken off life support to die the next day. When life support was removed, he did not die. He woke up and is alive and well to this day. I have laid hands on the stomach of a woman who was told to abort her child because the ultrasound showed the baby would have horrible birth defects. I heard the Holy Spirit say, "It is done," and God had the last word in the life of the beautiful baby born perfectly healthy. I have many times been in a financial situation where I thought I had nowhere to turn, but I prayed to God, reminded Him of the promises in His Word, and witnessed the matter being taken care of the very same day. If I were to give the full testimonies of answered prayers in my life and those whom I have taught the truth of God's Word on the matter, it would take volumes of books to do justice to the matter.

As a teacher in the Body of Christ, I give you the correct teaching according to scriptures. You as the believer have to decide to follow the Word of God. The enemy will do all that he possibly can to turn you away from the truth so that your prayers are hindered. He knows that your effectual prayers are a danger to the kingdom of this world. Take the time to not only read, but also study the different areas that we have gone over in the book. Meditate on the Word that is provided in each section. Implement the illustrations given through God's Word. Soon you will see the power of God working through your prayers and the very environment around you will start to shift. Soon you will fully understand that answered prayer is not only a right for every believer but also a weapon against the forces of evil that are coming against you and yours.

I want to encourage all that have been in a struggle with their prayer life, and did not understand why. Be encouraged. We learn through experience and the Word of God that the enemy will fight that which is a threat to his kingdom. He wants us to be in a place where we have given up and our prayers are ineffectual because they have been established on deceptive traditions that he has interjected into the Christian churches as deception to keep us from the truth. He wants us to believe that praying does not work to shatter our confidence in God and His Word. The truth is that the devil is a perpetrator of lies. **God is an answerer of prayers today in the same way He has always been. God has not changed; we just have to line up with Him.**

Ps 138:2-3
2 I will worship toward thy holy temple, and praise thy name for thy lovingkindness and for thy truth: for thou hast magnified thy word above all thy name.
3 In the day when I cried thou answeredst me, and strengthenedst me with strength in my soul.
KJV

Be Blessed and Be Encouraged.

Chapter 7

Praying in the Spirit
(An excerpt from "The Armor of God")

Sidenote: I am adding this chapter on praying in the Spirit, which is an excerpt from my earlier books "Assault On Innocence" and its excerpt "The Armor of God." This is a powerful teaching that will take you even deeper in your understanding on prayer.

The last part of the armor is actually not part of the armor at all. However, it might be the most important piece of information to allow you to effectively use the armor to protect yourself and your loved ones. It is the orders from the captain of the host. It's the classified intelligence from the front lines, along with surveillance of the enemy's movements. This type of praying is the line of communication that brings Intel on the war. We have already had a thorough teaching on the proper way to pray, but praying in the Spirit takes your prayer to another level.

Eph 6:18
18 Praying always with all prayer and supplication in the Spirit, and watching thereunto with all perseverance and supplication for all saints;
KJV

There are two points I want to emphasize on praying in the Spirit. Scholars disagree on the meaning of the verse above. Some say it is talking about praying in tongues; others think it is about the Holy Spirit taking over one's prayer and addressing subjects we are not aware of in the language we normally speak. Both of these things are accurate manifestations of the Spirit through us, but the question is, which one is Paul imploring us to do?

Before we dive into unraveling Paul's meaning, it is paramount that you have a proper understanding of the makeup of man. You need to have a precise understanding of Adam's makeup before and after the fall. God created Adam as a triune being. As we studied earlier, triune means he has three parts. We are spirit, soul, and body. You have no idea how many scriptures are misinterpreted, because scholars did not have the spiritual understanding of the makeup of man. Let me share an example with you.

1 John 3:9
9 Whosoever is born of God doth not commit sin; for his seed remaineth in him: and he cannot sin, because he is born of God.
KJV

This scripture is perplexing to most Christians, because we know even after we accept Christ that we still struggle with sin. So how is it that John is saying those born of God do not sin? I have heard Christians say that they cannot sin because they are born of God. Therefore, they believe when they do sin, it is not sinning. This is how false doctrine gets into the church, through misinterpretation of scripture.

John understands that we have spirit, soul, and flesh. God creates the flesh. God creates the soul. The spirit is not created. The spirit man is the part of us that is born of God. It is God's seed in our spirit, and our spirit man cannot sin.

1 Peter 3:4
4 But let it be the hidden man of the heart, in **that which is not corruptible**, even the ornament of a meek and quiet **spirit**, which is in the sight of God of great price.
KJV.

1 Peter 1:23
23 **Being born again, not of corruptible seed, but of incorruptible, by the word of God**, which liveth and abideth for ever. (KJV)

Your spirit man cannot sin, so when scripture says those who are born again do not sin, it is not you, it is your spirit. **When the Holy Spirit and your spirit becomes one, you are born again.** This is what Christ meant by those who are born again are like the wind blowing through the trees. You can feel them but cannot see them. When Adam sinned his spirit died, and that is the spirit in us that is born again (reborn) on confession and belief (from the heart) in Christ. The spirit does not die a natural death. Spiritual death is when our soul is separated from our spirit. This separation causes our soul, heart, and mind to have no access to the spirit realm.

To get to a deeper level of understanding, it is imperative that we as Christians learn to recognize when scripture is speaking to specific parts of our makeup or to the whole. We saw earlier in the book how Christ spoke of the three measures of meal as a metaphor for the three parts of the body and how the Holy Spirit brings about change in each part by our faith. Paul also addresses this spiritual purification, indicating the state we are to be found in upon Christ's return.

1 Thess 5:23
23 And the very God of peace **sanctify you wholly**; and I pray God **your whole spirit and soul and body** be preserved blameless unto the coming of our Lord Jesus Christ.
KJV

When we have the proper understanding of scripture, it will open up our spiritual understanding. This allows our wisdom to attain a higher level on the things of God.

The Groaning

I like giving testimonies of the things I have experienced in my Christian walk. These testimonies are actually a weapon of warfare. Scripture says we overcome the enemy by the blood of the Lamb and the word of our testimony:

Rev 12:11

11 And they overcame him by the blood of the Lamb, and **by the word of their testimony;** and they loved not their lives unto the death.

KJV

One of the reasons that I have acquired much knowledge on different subjects is because I share what I have. My understanding is that I have pieces of a puzzle and other believers have pieces also. We have some pieces different, and some are the same. When I share my testimony and knowledge with others, I am actually cloning my pieces and giving them to others. When I listen to the testimony of others, they are doing the same to me. So many times I have heard testimonies and received gems of knowledge that were the pieces of missing information needed to complete an important understanding that I had been toiling with.

Let me share my testimony on the groaning. I do not remember the first time it happened, but I do know how it happened. I was crying out to God and distraught about something I was going through. I mean real supplications.

It got to the point where I was just broken and did not know what to say to God. All of a sudden, deep from within me, a deep groan resonated through my body. I did not hear it. I just felt it. If you have ever had your heart broken, then you know the feeling. You can remember lying in bed and feeling this pain in your core that was hard to explain because you were not hurt physically but you felt internal pain. If you have experienced this, then it will be easy to get a grasp of what I am revealing. That hurtful pain was inward because it had no connection, so it just resonated inside you. I was not in physical pain, but it was real pain because my soul was hurting. When you are saved your spirit is quickened, and you are once again connected to God. When you feel that pain now, your soul is hurting but your spirit man gives the pain an antenna to transmit to God. Like a child crying out to his father, your spirit conveys the pain in your soul and cries out to God. It resonates through the spirit realm like a pulsing signal sent through space. It is one of the most hurtful feelings, yet beautiful because it gives us an understanding of our spiritual connection to our Father.

It went on for a couple of minutes, and then stopped. I noticed a change in the atmosphere after the groaning stopped, and I felt a calmness in my spirit. I did not know then, but I recognize now that it stopped because God answered. I knew that there was communication with God happening at that moment.. I just could not explain it. It was later on that I ran across Rom 8:26 and understood what happened. I also found out that many other Christians have experienced the same thing. This experience is also confirmation of a relationship with God. Here is a key to understanding this and resolving the question of praying in the spirit. We do not control the groaning. It is triggered by deep emotions and enabled by the Holy Spirit.

Rom 8:26-27
26 Likewise the Spirit also helpeth our infirmities: for we know not what we should pray for as we ought: but **the Spirit itself maketh intercession for us with groanings which cannot be uttered.**
27 And he that searcheth the hearts knoweth what is the mind of the Spirit, because he maketh intercession for the saints according to the will of God.
KJV

The Holy Spirit "maketh intercessions", meaning He intercedes on our behalf with the Father. It is important for you to understand that we do not control it, and we cannot make it happen anytime we want. The Holy Spirit looks at the circumstances, and He decides to intercede for us. Now ask yourself this question, when Paul tells us to pray in the Spirit, as the last part of the armor (Eph 6:18), who is he indicating controls it? Let us make it a little plainer.

How did Peter and Jude speak the same things? I was perplexed trying to understand how 2 Peter 2 and the book of Jude could be so similar. Many scholars teach that 2nd Peter plagiarized Jude or vice versa. As a believer, I rejected their understanding noting that most so-called scholars do not even believe the truth of the Bible. I knew there was an explanation so I prayed and asked God. At this time in my life, I started noticing that I would teach Bible study lessons, and then experience the same message being preached in church. Sometimes the preacher would even repeat the exact words that I had spoken. I have even witnessed a visiting pastor preach a whole message that was almost (word for word) the lesson I taught the day before. I was overjoyed when this happened because some of the things God was showing me were rewriting the understanding of many things taught traditionally. It would confirm my teachings to my Bible study group who were sometimes resistant to what I taught them, because it went against what they had previously been taught. I provided the Scriptures to confirm what I was teaching, but it was hard to uproot the false doctrine they had received before they started attending the Bible study. My teaching would be confirmed the next time they went to church. I realized that this was the doing of the Holy Spirit. In my mind, I believed the preachers and I were receiving the same teaching to deliver to God's people. I was about to find out that it went a lot deeper than that.

I was sitting in church, and the Holy Spirit said one word to me. Pray! I started praying, and when I was finished, I heard the pastor say, "Let's pray!" I was shocked. The pastor repeated my prayer word for word. I mean every single word! I finally understood what Christ meant:

Mark 13:11
11 But when they shall lead you, and deliver you up, take no thought beforehand what ye shall speak, neither do ye premeditate: but whatsoever shall be given you in that hour, that speak ye: **for it is not ye that speak, but the Holy Ghost.**
KJV

Finally, I knew how Peter and Jude could write the same thing. I also understood how I could teach a message, come to church, and hear the same message preached. This is a critical understanding that shines a light on how God speaks through us, and we do not even know it. Do you realize how many people have been deceived into not accepting the Gospel by naysayers that have no understanding of how these spiritual things work? Scholars telling people that because Peter and Jude wrote the same thing, it shows the epistles copied from each other and were not the Word of God. Let's not even mention all the controversy by the similarities of the gospels (books). I tell people that you cannot believe what scholars, who do not have any relationship with God, (some are atheist) conclude about the Bible. They have no spiritual understanding and cannot unravel the things of God. Therefore, they mislead the naïve people that are exposed to the foolery they speak.

2 Tim 3:7
7 Ever learning, and never able to come to the knowledge of the truth.
KJV

Therefore, we must conclude that if the Holy Spirit can speak through us, He can surely pray through us. Praying in the Spirit can mean the Holy Spirit utilizing us as vessels to bring about a needed prayer. Brothers and sisters, this happens to us all the time when we are in relationship with God. This is why the Holy Spirit will prompt us to pray, and we will not even know why. God sees something that is going to happen, and He needs us to trust Him, get down on our knees, and pray when He prompts.

We have one problem. Some of the times when the Holy Spirit is speaking through us, we have no idea, and we definitely do not control it. When Paul tells us to pray in the Spirit and assigns it with the Armor of God, he is telling us to do something that we control. Paul was not talking about the Holy Spirit praying through us. Paul was telling the believer to pray in tongues, and I can prove it.

As a child, I watched a movie, Chariots of Fire, where runners were trying to break the 4-minute mile mark. Scientists were coming up with reasons why it was impossible for men to run faster than a 4-minute mile. They actually came up with scientific proof that if a man ran faster than a 4 min mile he would probably die. A sub 4-minute mile was thought of as scientifically impossible, then someone broke it, and they all looked foolish. People have a way of coming up with theories to support their argument to make it seem like they are right when they are all wrong. I have already shown how many scholars are ignorant of spiritual things, because they are non-believers and their ideology leads to misinterpreting the scriptures. Well, the same mindset is happening in the church when it comes to understanding praying in the Spirit, which I am going to show means praying in tongues.

I have had ministers tell me that when Jude speaks about praying in the Holy Ghost, he is not talking about praying in tongues because he used capital S with Spirit showing it is the Holy Spirit praying. When Paul talks about praying in tongues, he uses the small s, which shows it is our spirit praying, and not the Holy Ghost. The problem is neither Paul nor Jude used a capital S because the concept of using a capital S to signify the Holy Spirit did not exist when they wrote the epistles. The capital S in Spirit, when signifying the Holy Spirit, is a modern concept not used by the writers of the Epistles. The writers knew that those who they sent the Epistles to understood clearly, which spirit they were designating. Spirit (Holy Spirit) or spirit (our spirit)! Therefore, we cannot use a modern method of translation to justify the belief one way or the other. What I want to show is that when we are speaking in tongues and our spirit is praying, the Holy Spirit is still involved in the process. So when Jude speaks of the Holy Spirit praying and Paul speaks of our spirit praying, both are speaking of the exact same thing.

Acts 2:4
4 And they were all filled with the Holy Ghost, and began to speak with other tongues, as **the Spirit gave them utterance**.
KJV

In Acts 2:4, we see that the men were speaking in other tongues. The Holy Spirit gave the ability for the utterance to occur. The Holy Spirit is what enables our spirit to speak through us. Furthermore, we see Jude telling us to pray in the Holy Ghost, alluding to the fact that we are the controlling force in the process. I have already shown that when we speak and the Holy Spirit is speaking through us, we do not control it. Most Christians are not even aware of when the Holy Spirit is speaking through them. Therefore, we know Jude could not have been telling us to pray in the Spirit meaning that the Holy Ghost is praying.

Jude 18-23
18 How that they told you there should be mockers in the last time, who should walk after their own ungodly lusts.
19 These be they who separate themselves, sensual, having not the Spirit.

20 But ye, beloved, **building up yourselves on your most holy faith, praying in the Holy Ghost,**
21 Keep yourselves in the love of God, looking for the mercy of our Lord Jesus Christ unto eternal life.
22 And of some have compassion, making a difference:
23 And others save with fear, pulling them out of the fire; hating even the garment spotted by the flesh.
KJV

When we pray in tongues, the Holy Spirit is giving us the ability to do it, but our spirit is praying. Who is in control when our spirit prays?

1 Cor 14:32
32 And the spirits of the prophets are subject to the prophets.
KJV

I understand that many who are reading this book have never spoken in tongues. Some of you have even been programmed to believe that the gifts of the Holy Spirit do not exist anymore. Read the next sentence carefully. **They have lied to you.** The gift of the Spirit is still available to every believer in Christ. The gift was not temporary, neither was it only for a select few.

Acts 2:38-39
38 Then Peter said unto them, Repent, and be baptized every one of you in the name of Jesus Christ for the remission of sins, and **ye shall receive the gift of the Holy Ghost.**
39 For the promise is unto you, and to your children, and **to all that are afar off,** even **as many as the Lord our God shall call.**
KJV

I want to say this loud and clear: The baptism of the Holy Spirit (gift), along with the individual gifts, is available to all believers. Remember, Paul reveals that those who are afar off are the Gentiles. Peter also adds that the gift of the Holy Spirit is to all that God is calling to salvation. If you are called, then the gift is for you.

I have been teaching a Bible study group for 17 years where 75% of the members have received the baptism of the Holy Spirit after they started attending the Bible study. When I say 75%, I mean those who operate in the gifts of the Holy Spirit. I would be surprised if more than 5% of those who identify themselves as Christians today have received the baptism of the Holy Spirit and operate in the gifts. So why is it that so many have not received the baptism? It is a free gift, and it comes through your faith. Once you confess with your mouth **AND** believe in your heart, you will receive the gift. This is a promise from God, and He keeps His promises.

If you have confessed Christ and have not received the baptism as of yet, then check your belief. Ask God to search you and show you the problem. Sometimes it is as simple as asking Him. If you have yet to receive the baptism of the Holy Spirit, I need you to read the below verses carefully.

Luke 11:9-13
9 And I say unto you, **Ask, and it shall be given you**; seek, and ye shall find; knock, and it shall be opened unto you.
10 For **every one that asketh receiveth**; and **he that seeketh findeth;** and to him that knocketh it shall be opened.
11 If a son shall ask bread of any of you that is a father, will he give him a stone? or if he ask a fish, will he for a fish give him a serpent?
12 Or if he shall ask an egg, will he offer him a scorpion?
13 **If ye then, being evil, know how to give good gifts unto your children: how much more shall your heavenly Father give the Holy Spirit to them that ask him?**
KJV

So what exactly is Christ telling us in those verses? Everyone who asks for the gift (who's in right relationship with God) is going to receive it, and He is talking about the Holy Ghost. Everyone! Therefore, your first step after confession and belief in your heart is to ask for the Holy Spirit. (Please reread the chapters on prayer to make sure you are praying right.) In addition, you have to believe! Ask yourself this question: Why did Christ say, "If he shall ask an egg, will he offer him a scorpion?" Christ does not want us to be afraid of receiving the gift of the Holy Spirit. The Holy Spirit does not operate in an environment of fear. Fear exposes a lack of faith and without faith, we receive nothing from God. Many believing Christians have not received the Holy Spirit because of fear! The enemy uses fear of the unknown such as speaking in tongues to cancel out peoples' faith. No faith, no gift!

When I get new members to the Bible study that have confessed Christ but have yet to receive the baptism of the Holy Spirit, they receive simple instructions. Read every scripture in the Bible dealing with the Holy Spirit. I mean search out every single mention of the Holy Spirit directly or indirectly and read it. Study those scriptures alone until you receive the Holy Spirit. Examine nothing else but those scriptures until you receive. Continually pray and ask God for the gift. That means every time you pray mention it to God. Christ taught us to be persistent in petitioning God. Remember the gift is free to all those who confess and believe. How do you know you believe? You will want to walk according to the will of God.

Do not let naysayers come and tell you why you do not need the gift, or that it is not available anymore. They have not received because their own words are killing their faith. How can you receive something that you confess doesn't exist, or you confess you don't need it? These same naysayers will come and talk you into agreeing with them, and kill your faith in God's promise. **Never let the words that you do not need the baptism come out of your mouth, NEVER!**

The reason I warn about naysayers is that the enemy knows the power of the gift of the Holy Spirit. He will use everything in his control to hinder you from receiving the gift. Some will get a feeling of fear that is being generated by the enemy to set up doubt in their heart. I have also seen many churches with false teachings that hinder their members from receiving the gift. To make it into the kingdom of God, you will need everything that God has appointed for you in this life. These tools assist us in enduring to the end to achieve eternal life in New Jerusalem. Ask (in the right manner), and you will receive. He promised, and God keeps His promises.

Praying in Tongues

It is important for you to understand that praying in tongues is incorporated in the gift of tongues. Many people believe they are different or they are talking about the same thing. Let me try and give you a better understanding of the difference between the two. Everyone who has their spirit quickened (come alive) will have the ability of their spirit speaking through them. This is a litmus test to know if your spirit is alive. When you are in a situation of stress or agony, your spirit will speak through you. We even have an example in Scripture that many people miss. When Christ was in the garden of Gethsemane about to be crucified, he spoke to the Father, and it was Christ the spirit speaking. His Spirit was crying out to the Father.

Mark 14:35-36
35 And he went forward a little, and fell on the ground, and prayed that, if it were possible, the hour might pass from him.
36 And he said, **Abba, Father**, all things are possible unto thee; take away this cup from me: nevertheless not what I will, but what thou wilt.
KJV

       Do you realize that nowhere else in Scripture does Christ say ABBA? Now I want you to read carefully what Paul wrote about the Holy Spirit and our spirits crying out to God.

Rom 8:15-17
15 For ye have not received the spirit of bondage again to fear; but ye have received the Spirit of adoption, **whereby we cry**, *Abba, Father*.
16 **The Spirit itself beareth witness with our spirit**, that we are the children of God:
17 And if children, then heirs; heirs of God, and joint-heirs with Christ; **if so be that we suffer with him**, that we may be also glorified together.
KJV

Gal 4:6-7
6 And **because ye are sons**, God hath sent forth **the Spirit of his Son into your hearts, crying, Abba, Father.**
7 Wherefore thou **art no more a servant, but a son**; and if a son, then an heir of God through Christ.
KJV

The scripture says by at least two or three witnesses let everything be established. The Holy Spirit and our spirit bear witness that we have become children of God. God is not a Father of souls or flesh; He is the Father of spirits. If your spirit is not alive, then God is not your Father. Yes harsh, but I would rather sober you with a hard truth than appease you to death and hell with a lie.

Heb 12:9

9 Furthermore we have had fathers of our flesh which corrected us, and we gave them reverence: shall we not much rather **be in subjection unto the Father of spirits, and live?**
KJV

Both the Holy Spirit and your spirit can speak through your body. The Holy Spirit gives us the capability to speak in tongues and pray in tongues. Depending on the source of the message (Holy Spirit / Your spirit), the feeling is entirely different. I can pray in the spirit (tongues) at anytime. It is just me allowing my spirit to have a verbal communion with God. My spirit addresses the spiritual things happening around me that I might not be aware of, because they cannot be seen.

Yet, when the Father through the Holy Spirit speaks through me, it is as if every molecule in my body is about to explode. In this case, it is God bringing a message through me that usually requires interpretation. We do not control when the Holy Spirit speaks through us, and although we **can** shut it down, this comes with effort. When Paul and Jude are advising the believers to pray in tongues to edify themselves, they are speaking about allowing your spirit to pray. Remember, the capability to bring forth the utterance comes by way of the Holy Spirit, but the message is coming from your spirit man.

Many years ago, I attended a church where the gift of tongues was demonstrated almost every service. You would hear someone speaking in tongues, or a minister would bring a message to the congregation. The level of understanding of the gift was very limited in the congregation. One summer we had a well-known international ministry visit our church. They spent the whole weekend going out into the community doing outreach. They were good at what they did because the service held at the church was packed with visitors. One of the guest ministers was teaching the congregation that believers could speak in tongues anytime they wanted. The assistant pastor came, took the mic, and sat the minister down. I felt so embarrassed for the church. The assistant pastor thought the minister was trying to teach people how to talk in tongues, but I realized that was not what the minister was doing. It was a misunderstanding enabled by ignorance.

Many believers have received the baptism of the Holy Spirit, with the evidence of speaking in tongues, and yet have never spoken again. Others believe you need to be hyped up to speak in tongues. Let me share with you how I found out the truth.

It took a long time for me to receive the gift of tongues. I had actually been teaching biblical studies in a small group for over a year; members of the group had received the baptism, and I had not. I would watch new people come to the group, receive the teaching, and get the baptism of the Holy Spirit with the evidence of speaking in tongues while I had never spoken. I was studying and praying for the gift. I had visions, prayed with people who were healed and delivered, yet had never spoken. One night while teaching the small group of eight individuals, something happened. We were all sitting at the dining room table. I was at the head of the table with three people on my right, three to my left, and another directly in front of me. We were a group of young people seeking hard for the kingdom, who met every Saturday night. God had just appointed me as the leader of the group by first speaking to me, then to the young woman that was leading the group before me.

It was the end of the Bible study, and we were about to close. While sitting at the table; the person to my immediate right spoke a word about speaking in tongues. He then quickly looked over at me realizing that I had been struggling to receive the gift. He looked at me apologetically, because he did not want to offend or prick me with his words. I looked at him and smiled but never said a word. In my thoughts, I said, "It's fine, when God is ready for me to speak I will speak." All of a sudden, I felt a tingling in my belly and then it felt like every molecule in my body exploded. A great breath of air burst out of my mouth, and I started speaking in tongues. I am not talking about chirping, stuttering, or the repeating of the same words. It was clearly another language being spoken, and I knew it was God bringing a message through me. I also realized that I was speaking to each individual in the room starting to my left, and going around clockwise. I cannot explain how I knew, but I knew it was a message being spoken into the spirit of each of them. When I got to one young lady, the words became loud and the tone harsh. She fell off her chair and started crying. She would tell me later that she was being chastised for something, but she never told me what it was. I moved on to the next person, and the tone went back to gentle and comforting. After I had spoken to each individual, the power surge I felt in my body subsided, and I stopped speaking. Everyone just sat there amazed.

I got out of my chair and walked around the corner from the dining room to a hallway. I leaned against the wall with my arms uplifted and wept. I knew it was the Father speaking through me. I was broken, and I spoke what was in my heart. I said, "But Father, I wanted to speak to you." I heard a small gentle voice say, "Just speak." When I opened my mouth, I burst into tongues again but it was different. It was powerful but did not come with the surge of power and my molecules on fire. It was just bursting out of me, and although I could not understand the words, I knew without a shadow of a doubt that it was me telling God everything! I felt like a little child who had not seen his father in a very long time, and when he came home, he went to his father weeping. He then told him everything he always wanted to tell him. I spoke for about a half hour. When I was done, I was the happiest I had ever been in my life.

Later that night when I got home, I dove into the scriptures to get a better understanding of everything that had taken place. When I read these verses, I got puzzled:

1 Cor 14:14-15
14 For **if I pray in an unknown tongue, my spirit prayeth**, but my understanding is unfruitful.
15 What is it then? **I will pray with the spirit, and I will pray with the understanding also:** I will sing with the spirit, and I will sing with the understanding also. (KJV)

I was like, "Wait a minute." If Paul is saying he prays in tongues, doesn't that mean he can control when he goes into tongues? See, every time I observed people speaking in tongues, it looked like they were energized, and the power of God just dropped on them, and they went into tongues. My understanding from what I was reading was that Paul just knelt down and prayed in tongues. Well, I did not know any better, so I got off my bed, got on my knees, and just started praying in tongues. I would pray for a while, stop, and then pray for a while in English. This went on for about an hour.

When I finished praying, I called one of the members of the Bible study who already spoke in tongues and asked them if they could speak in tongues anytime they wanted. Her name was Joanne, and she had been speaking in tongues longer than all of us. She told me, "No, I can't." I asked her if she ever tried. She replied, "No!" I asked her to try and she said, "Ok." I could hear her start praising God in an attempt to bring it on. I stopped her and said, "Joanne, just speak." She burst into tongues. She was shocked. She had no idea that she could just speak whenever she wanted. I quickly said, "Goodbye," and called another person who spoke in tongues. It was Lemuel. I asked him the same question, if he could speak in tongues anytime he wanted. He also replied that he could not. I again asked if he had ever tried and he said, "No." I asked him to try and he burst into tongues. I called two other people with the same results. Then I called an older brother in the church and asked him if he could. I was surprised by his answer. He said, "I don't know." Wow! I then realized that he was the only one that was opened-minded. Everyone else said, "No" because that is what they had been taught over the years. They never questioned what they were told; they just accepted it and never tried. The brother I was talking to now was actually at church. When he tried to speak and went into tongues, he started running around the parking lot praising God. I really think he understood what this meant and was overjoyed with learning something new.

So that was when I realized that you could speak in tongues and pray in tongues and you do not have to call down heaven to do it. The church I was attending was teaching that we could only speak when God has a message to bring to the church. I am always amazed at how adamant people can be even when they are wrong. God has really worked on me in the area of just speaking the truth, leaving the seed, and moving on when people reject it. Funny thing about a seed is you can drop it in some dirt, come back every day, and see nothing. Nevertheless, let some rain fall and see how quickly it germinates and starts to grow.

Let me share another experience I had with someone who rejected biblical teaching on the Holy Spirit. I was working with a very strong Christian, which made it a joy to go to work and fellowship with her. She had some powerful testimonies that were a blessing to my Christian walk. One day I shared with her my teaching on the truth of believers having the capability to pray in tongues whenever they wanted to. She totally rejected it and told me I was wrong and teaching false doctrine. I had a lot of respect for her so what she said was hurtful. The debate got heated, so I ended it by telling her the next time she prays just go into tongues and she will be able to confirm what scripture says. The discussion ended there, and nothing more was mentioned on the subject.

A few months went by, and we worked together occasionally. One particular day while working together she asked if I remembered the day we discussed praying in tongues. I stated, "Yes." She then told me she went home, and even though she had rejected what I said, she prayed and tried it. She said, "You were right Williams, I went straight into tongues." Every single person that has the gift, whom I have spoken to about this and has actually tried it, has gone into tongues.

This knowledge is fought against in many churches because the enemy does not want you to have access to the power in your prayer language. He knows how important the spiritual lines of communication are in this war. He wants you to have as little access to it as possible. Sadly, many inexperienced and unlearnt Christians fight against the truth of praying in tongues.

Now let's get back to understanding why praying in tongues is so important. Your spirit, which is one with the Holy Spirit, knows more about what is going on than you do. I remember when preachers used to preach that the reason the gift of tongues was given was because the devil could not understand it. They believed it would enable us to speak to God without the enemy knowing what was being said. The Bible says tongues are a language, and when the disciples spoke in tongues on Pentecost, onlookers understood those who spoke in their native tongue. So when Satan goes to Russia, does he call for an interpreter? Does he carry translators with him when he goes from nation to nation? Scripture also says when we speak in tongues it can be the heavenly language. Did they change the heavenly language when Satan and his angels were cast down? Do you see the problem with the teaching that the devil does not understand tongues? The devil knows the language of heaven and every language spoken by men. Do not let anyone fool you.

1 Cor 13:1
13:1 Though I speak with **the tongues of men and of angels**, and have not charity, I am become as sounding brass, or a tinkling cymbal.
KJV

So why do we pray in tongues? There is information that God wants to share within our spirit that He does not want **us** to know. Let us examine some of the most famous verses in Scripture taken from the love chapter of the Bible. I want to clarify the understanding.

1 Cor 13:9-13
9 For **we know in part, and we prophesy in part.**
10 But when that which is perfect is come, then that which is in part shall be done away.
11 When I was a child, I spake as a child, I understood as a child, I thought as a child: but when I became a man, I put away childish things.
12 For now we see through a glass, darkly; but then face to face: now I know in part; but then shall I know even as also I am known.
13 And now abideth faith, hope, charity, these three; but the greatest of these is charity.
KJV

I have heard too many different interpretations on these verses to even try to comment on all of them. Paul was specific in what he was saying and there should not be any controversy in the understanding. Paul is talking about spiritual growth, which starts with our faith and ends when we are completely walking in love. He is saying that as children in Christ, we know in part because God knows we cannot be trusted. Think about walking into church and knowing everything about everyone in the building. Could God trust you to know everything about them but still love them and treat them the same? Mature Christians who have put on Christ (His image), will be operating in love. Mature Christians know God used some men in the Bible that did some ungodly things before they came to the knowledge of the truth. As my good friend Pastor Garland would say, **"You have to look past their sins so you can see their needs."** As babes in Christ, we are judgmental of others and it hinders us from being vessels God can use to minister to broken people. As mature Christians, we understand God's process of changing them so He can be glorified. For example, there are some people reading this book that when I was a babe in Christ, if I knew your history, I might have been reluctant to deliver a message (or teaching) to you. Likewise, some of you, if you knew me before I came to Christ, you might not want to listen to anything I have to say. **Love removes all the roadblocks that stop us from receiving and presenting God's message.** So Paul is expounding on the fact that as babes in Christ we can only be trusted with knowing in part and prophesying in part. When we grow in love, God is able to share more knowledge of things with us! The fullness of love (perfection) will enable us to know even as God knows.

Many times God has sent people to me with messages that they did not understand about something I was going through at the time. He did not want to expose the issue because He knew their level of love. If God told some of us, what our brothers and sisters were going through we would blast it all through the media. Everyone would know hours after God told us. We cannot be trusted. If you take time to research those who received revelations in the Bible, you will find that Daniel and John received the most. Daniel was called the man greatly beloved and John was mentioned, as the one Christ loved. Why were they so greatly loved by the Father and Christ? Daniel and John loved the most. Daniel said the prayer for the nation he loved that turned the captivity of Judah, and John was the apostle that stayed with Christ before, during, and after

His death when the others had fled. **Those who love the most are trusted with more revelation than those who do not.**

Paul is showing that as we grow in love from spiritual childhood to spiritual adulthood, we put on the image of Christ. Those who have put on the image are those who enter into perfection (Christ is perfection). We will no longer be as babes who cannot be trusted but Christ-like. God will share with us the mysteries of the kingdom and He will speak plainly to us about all things. Remember the Breastplate of Righteousness is also called the Breastplate of Faith and Love. When you move from your initial faith to walking in love, you have achieved righteousness. You are more than just covered by Christ's righteousness you have entered into His righteousness. You have put on Christ!

Until then you cannot be trusted to know everything. Therefore, God will have a conversation with your spirit in tongues, sharing information to help guide you in secret because you cannot yet be trusted. There are also things He will speak into your spirit that He hides from you to keep you from walking in pride. You don't believe me? Let me prove it to you.

Job 33:14-18
14 For God speaketh once, yea twice, **yet man perceiveth it not**.
15 In a dream, in a vision of the night, when deep sleep falleth upon men, in slumberings upon the bed;
16 **Then he openeth the ears of men, and sealeth their instruction,**
17 That he may withdraw man from his purpose, and hide pride from man.
18 He keepeth back his soul from the pit, and his life from perishing by the sword.
KJV

Nothing has changed. God still speaks into us when we are not aware. He guides us into things and away from things. He protects us from our own selves and emotions. He speaks His purpose into our lives.

You are praying one day at home and all of a sudden, you burst into tongues. When you are done, you get no interpretation and you wonder what happened. Your spirit was responding to God about the car accident you are going to get into because God needs you to go to the hospital. When you get there, you are in a room with someone who is not only terminally ill but also has a first class ticket to hell. Now, God wants to void that ticket and offer the person salvation. He knows the person had a bad childhood experience with a Christian and does not want to hear anything a Christian has to say. God knows if a Christian enters the room broken and injured, it will be enough to bring down the wall of resistance and allow the Gospel to reach the person's heart. Therefore, you enter the room, the person feels sorry for your condition and opens up to you, and you are able to share the Gospel and lead the person to Christ. God knows you and knows if He tells you that He has assigned you to go through a horrible accident to reach a lost soul, 12 hours later, in order to stop the storm from sinking the cruise ship you boarded to Jamaica, they will be throwing you overboard. Yes, you will be the modern day Jonah!

There is another reason why we pray in tongues. Sometimes when I am praying for a person I get the premonition that I need to pray in tongues. For those who do not know, sometimes when people pray in tongues they will know the subject matter yet do not understand the words. I have prayed for people, went into tongues, and knew my spirit was addressing them being bound up in sexual sins. God knew it would be an embarrassment to the person, so He would not guide my prayer into fornication but would guide me into tongues to address the matter. When you are praying in a group, the Holy Spirit will address the issues in the private life of individuals and will not expose them to the group. This is why tongues are used instead of prophecy.

We serve a loving God who understands our temptations and our struggles. He wants us to turn from our sins and gives us every opportunity (with longsuffering) before He exposes us to the public. This is the example given to us when our brethren have wronged us. We first take the matter to them in private. If they refuse to hear us, then we take a witness. If they refuse to hear the witness, then we bring the matter before the whole church. There have been many times when I am teaching and the Holy Spirit will guide me into addressing certain sins. I will know that someone in the group is struggling with the sin but the person will not be identified. God is protecting them from the embarrassment because He knows it can harm their spiritual growth. The God we serve is gentle and loving. He wants the best for His children. It is not to say that God will never expose someone because if the person continues to reject the call for repentance, then God will expose the situation to bring him or her to a decision. Therefore, speaking in tongues can also be a way of protecting those who God is calling to repentance by God dealing with the matter privately unknown to others.

Finally, I want you to understand that there will be times when you feel something is wrong but you cannot put your finger on it. You will wake up in the middle of the night with someone on your mind, or just disturbed, and do not understand why. Pray in tongues. Your spirit along with the Holy Spirit will be able to pinpoint the problem even though you are dumbfounded about what your spirit is sensing. Many times while you are praying in tongues, you may have a vision or word of knowledge that will inform you of the situation. Whether you do or not, you can be assured that spiritually, the problem will be addressed. This is why the enemy of our souls fights against spiritual gifts so fervently. The gifts take the fight to the source, which originates in the spirit realm. We are given access to the planning realm of Satan. The Holy Spirit exposes demonic activity in its hiding place. In such a wicked age, the gift of tongues is desperately needed, yet the enemy has put forth such a powerful campaign against it that the very people who need it the most are not seeking after it. Sadly, some even speak against the very gift that they need to overcome the devices of the enemy, meanwhile Satan and his kingdom are laughing at them.

1 Cor 14:37-39

37 If any man think himself to be a prophet, or spiritual, let him acknowledge that the things that I write unto you are the commandments of the Lord.
38 But if any man be ignorant, let him be ignorant.
39 Wherefore, brethren, covet to prophesy, and forbid not to speak with tongues.
KJV

The Need for Salvation

If you are reading (or have read), this book and you do not know Christ Jesus as your personal Savior, all it takes is a simple prayer to change your circumstance and start you on the pathway to eternal life. Christ came and died in your place to save you from sin and eternal damnation. Do you understand why His death was necessary? God did not create the world to be wicked and to perish, but He did give all humanity freewill. When Adam sinned in disobeying God, it allowed wickedness to enter the world through sin. God has appointed a day to judge the wickedness of this world.

God loves the creation He has made. He sent his Son Jesus (Yehoshua) to redeem the earth and all those who believe (accept Christ and walk in His truth) that God sent His Son to die so that we all might live.

Christ's death and resurrection from the dead enables us to come back into relationship with the Father. He took the penalty of death for us to remove our sins, and bring us back into a right relationship with God. With a right relationship comes the renewal of our spirit, which allows us to sense and understand spiritual things. His resurrection represents our spiritual renewing and the hope of eternal life in God's Kingdom.

(Precious Bible Promises)

YOU ARE A SINNER...
Rom 3:10
10 As it is written, There is none righteous, no, not one:

1 John 1:8
8 If we say that we have no sin, we deceive ourselves, and the truth is not in us.

Rom 3:23
23 For all have sinned, and come short of the glory of God;

THERE IS A PRICE TO BE PAID FOR SIN...
Eph 5:3-7

3 But fornication, and all uncleanness, or covetousness, let it not be once named among you, as becometh saints;

4 Neither filthiness, nor foolish talking, nor jesting, which are not convenient: but rather giving of thanks.

5 For this ye know, that no whoremonger, nor unclean person, nor covetous man, who is an idolater, hath any inheritance in the kingdom of Christ and of God.

6 Let no man deceive you with vain words: for because of these things cometh the wrath of God upon the children of disobedience.

7 Be not ye therefore partakers with them.

Gal 5:19-21

19 Now the works of the flesh are manifest, which are these; Adultery, fornication, uncleanness, lasciviousness,

20 Idolatry, witchcraft, hatred, variance, emulations, wrath, strife, seditions, heresies,

21 Envyings, murders, drunkenness, revellings, and such like: of the which I tell you before, as I have also told you in time past, that they which do such things shall not inherit the kingdom of God.

1 Cor 6:9-10

9 Know ye not that the unrighteous shall not inherit the kingdom of God? Be not deceived: neither fornicators, nor idolaters, nor adulterers, nor effeminate, nor abusers of themselves with mankind,

10 Nor thieves, nor covetous, nor drunkards, nor revilers, nor extortioners, shall inherit the kingdom of God.

GOD TAKES NO PLEASURE IN ANYONE GOING TO HELL...
Ezek 33:11

11 Say unto them, As I live, saith the Lord GOD, I have no pleasure in the death of the wicked; but that the wicked turn from his way and live: turn ye, turn ye from your evil ways; for why will ye die, O house of Israel?

1 Tim 2:4

4 Who will have all men to be saved, and to come unto the knowledge of the truth.

NEED OF REPENTANCE...

2 Peter 3:9

9 The Lord is not slack concerning his promise, as some men count slackness; but is longsuffering to us-ward, not willing that any should perish, but that all should come to repentance.

Luke 5:32

32 I came not to call the righteous, but sinners to repentance.

Acts 3:19

19 Repent ye therefore, and be converted, that your sins may be blotted out, when the times of refreshing shall come from the presence of the Lord;

GOD LOVES YOU...

Rev 3:19-20

19 As many as I love, I rebuke and chasten: be zealous therefore, and repent.

20 Behold, I stand at the door, and knock: if any man hear my voice, and open the door, I will come in to him, and will sup with him, and he with me.

GOD SENT HIS SON JESUS TO SAVE YOU...

Matt 18:11

11 For the Son of man is come to save that which was lost.

John 3:16-18

16 For God so loved the world, that he gave his only begotten Son, that whosoever believeth in him should not perish, but have everlasting life.

17 For God sent not his Son into the world to condemn the world; but that the world through him might be saved.

18 He that believeth on him is not condemned: but he that believeth not is condemned already, because he hath not believed in the name of the only begotten Son of God.

CHRIST DIED FOR YOU AND WANTS TO SAVE YOU...

Rom 6:23

23 For the wages of sin is death; but the gift of God is eternal life through Jesus Christ our Lord.

Rom 5:6-8

6 For when we were yet without strength, in due time Christ died for the ungodly.

7 For scarcely for a righteous man will one die: yet peradventure for a good man some would even dare to die.

8 But God commendeth his love toward us, in that, while we were yet sinners, Christ died for us.

CHRIST CAN SAVE YOU NOW...

Rom 10:9-10

9 That if thou shalt confess with thy mouth the Lord Jesus, and shalt believe in thine heart that God hath raised him from the dead, thou shalt be saved.

10 For with the heart man believeth unto righteousness; and with the mouth confession is made unto salvation.

YOU CAN KNOW THAT YOU'RE SAVED...

1 John 5:10-13

10 He that believeth on the Son of God hath the witness in himself: he that believeth not God hath made him a liar; because he believeth not the record that God gave of his Son.

11 And this is the record, that God hath given to us eternal life, and this life is in his Son.

12 He that hath the Son hath life; and he that hath not the Son of God hath not life.

13 These things have I written unto you that believe on the name of the Son of God; that ye may know that ye have eternal life, and that ye may believe on the name of the Son of God.

A Sinner's Prayer...

Father, the Creator of all things, I come to You today and confess that I am a sinner. I confess that I believe that You sent your Son Christ Jesus to die for my sins to bring me back into relationship with You. I accept what He has done and repent for all my past sins. (Confess all pass sins that you can remember.) Forgive me Father, renew my spirit, and lead me in the way of righteousness. I ask this in the name of your Son Jesus Christ. AMEN!

Maranatha!

References

Fausset's Bible Dictionary, Electronic Database Copyright (c) 1998, 2003 by Biblesoft
International Standard Bible Encyclopaedia, Electronic Database Copyright © 1996, 2003 by Biblesoft, Inc. All rights reserved.)
Precious Bible Promises (From the New King James Version) (c) 1983 Thomas Nelson, Publishers.
David W. Bercot, Editor A Dictionary of Early Christian Beliefs. Peabody, Hendrickson Publisher, Inc. 1998
Williams Samuel, The Truth about the Tithe Copyright (c) 2016
Williams Samuel, Assault on Innocence Copyright (c) 2017

Other Books by this Author

Sleep Paralysis
Christmas and The Mark of The Beast
Hidden In The Garden
Hidden In The Metaphor (Excerpt from "Hidden In The Garden")
Assault On Innocence (Protecting the Children)
The Armor of God (A Deeper understanding) (Excerpt from "Assault On Innocence")
The Truth about the Tithe (Making Merchandise of God's People)
Curses and Tithes, Truth and Lies (Excerpt from "The Truth About the Tithes")

Note from the Author

Let Others Know!
If this book has been a blessing to you, please share the good news by visiting Amazon.com and leaving a positive review.
Your review is greatly appreciated. Thank you!
Let's Stay Connected!
If you would like to be placed on a contact list to be notified of future books, please email me at Samuelkem@aol.com.
Type "**Book Contact List**" in the subject line, include your name, **and email address in the email** itself. Thank you!

Made in the USA
Columbia, SC
18 June 2020